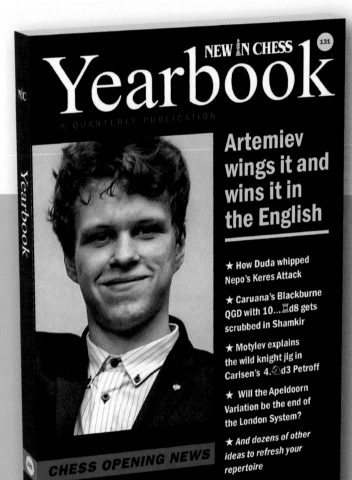

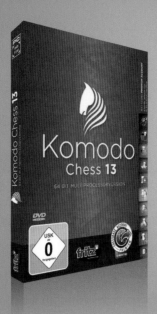

'Efficiency is intelligent laziness.'

**CONTRIBUTORS TO THIS ISSUE**
Erwin l'Ami, Jeroen Bosch, Maxim Dlugy, Anish Giri, Nils Grandelius, Pentala Harikrishna, John Henderson, Robert Hess, Gawain Jones, Vincent Keymer, Mihail Marin, Peter Heine Nielsen, Maxim Notkin, Arthur van de Oudeweetering, Judit Polgar, Matthew Sadler, Jan Timman

ALINA L'AMI

# Banned
# & Back

**I**ran has witnessed several revolutions in its history, and a most
fascinating recent one has been in chess — especially since the
game was banned under Ayatollah Khomeini's authoritative
rule during the 1979 Islamic revolution, that forced the country's
players to go underground with their boards and pieces.
Happily, the game is flourishing once again under a more moderate
administration, as witness this intense Tehran chess street-scene.
With the relaxation, the nation is also experiencing a mini
chess-boom. The Iranian chess federation now has one of the most
professional coaching centres, based in Tehran, regularly hiring
in international trainers and grandmasters to do the coaching. As
a result, Iranian children are now beginning to rival some of the
more dominant nations, such as India and China, in FIDE age-group
championships.
Iran, now with 15 GMs (and counting), is currently ranked world
number 24 by FIDE, ahead of more developed chess nations Sweden,
Denmark and Bulgaria. They also have a very youthful and strong
Olympiad squad, that's being built around rising teenage stars
Alireza Firouzja (15) and Parham Maghsoodloo (18), both of whom
are on the cusp of becoming the first Iranians to reach 2700. ■

## There's an app for that

Ever found yourself in a strange city and wondering where to find a place you can go and physically play a game of chess, or perhaps even view a chess landmark? Whether it be a chess club, street chess, giant chess, playing over a cup of coffee in a café, or even something a tad stronger in

**HACKNEY CHESS MEETUP**
📍 143-145 Stoke Newington High Street, N16, London, UNITED KINGDOM

I am here:

*In London on a Saturday? How about the legendary beer and blitz at The Rochester Castle?*

a bar? Then now, in the immortal words of the ubiquitous Apple advertising slogan, there's an app for that!

Parisian chess-loving developer 'Pierre' has created 'La Chess Connection', where, as it describes

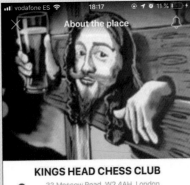

**KINGS HEAD CHESS CLUB**
📍 33 Moscow Road, W2 4AH, London, UNITED KINGDOM

I am here:

*Or do you prefer to wax nostalgic at the Kings Head on Moscow Road?*

in the App Store, you can 'Discover, meet, share and play', no matter where you are. It also allows you to list bars, clubs, historical places, and many other places associated with chess – the idea being to grow and connect a chess network.

And sure enough, on a recent visit to London, the app easily found our old haunt of the Kings Head Chess Club on the Moscow Road. The community around the app is expanding daily, with the latest cosmopolitan sites tagged being the Museum of the Central Chess Club in Moscow, the Haardstee Public Chess Table in Amsterdam, the Audubon Bar in Boston, and the Drunken Monkey in Hyderabad.

And best of all, the app is free!

## Hanging pawns

We've all heard of the chess term 'hanging pawns', but now a craftsman from Blieskastel in Germany has taken this to a more literal meaning by creating and marketing a chess coatrack where you can hang a coat or even a backpack on a pawn, or indeed any other piece for that matter.

Volker Rieck, of Creative Holtz, who gets lots of original ideas from discarded items he finds while wandering around flea markets, spotted this lovely wooden chess set and board with wonderful inlaid detailing... and then he had a sudden brainwave of how to upcycle the board and pieces into a useful everyday household item. After gluing and then screwing the pieces to the board, and simply adding a convenient shelf on top, Rieck created the novelty item of a chess-themed coatrack.

The chess coatrack and some of Riek's other wonderfully innovative creations can be purchased through his Etsy Shop. The one on display shows a Classical Caro-Kann Defence, but for an added price and a longer wait-time, Rieck is open

*Finally someone managed to peg it: that's what the solid Caro-Kann is for!*

to making bespoke chess-themed coatracks with any opening or position from a game on the board.

## Extinction Rebellion

Authorities in London were taken by surprise by a much larger-than-anticipated series of protests recently, led by British climate change group Extinction Rebellion (XR), who staged strategic demonstrations at a number of iconic sites that brought parts of central London to a prolonged standstill.

The Metropolitan Police say they were totally unprepared for the 'very new' type of protest, which saw thousands descend on London and occupy for 11 days some of the capital's busiest roads. There were more than 1,200 arrests during the protests, which begun on 15 April at Oxford Circus, Marble Arch, Piccadilly Circus, Waterloo Bridge and Parliament Square.

The very effective XR protest, which was purely peaceful and non-violent, was aimed to raise awareness of the escalating threat of runaway climate change. Worth fighting for, we thought – and we were taken by the sitting-round-the-campfire-singing-'Kumbaya'-spirit of the mainly young protestors, particularly the group who pulled out their hippy-themed blankets and cushions, placed them on the middle of the

Far from extinct: chess as a pleasant way to while away a sunny day.

Karpov Not Kasparov might have been Kasparov Not Karpov.

road at Parliament Square... and then, to the surprise of the police and the media, took out chess sets to challenge all comers to a game!

## Inseparable

We received a missive from Anthony Saidy. The retired physician and veteran International Master's medical and chess interests were simultaneously piqued by two new weighty tomes that featured in the February edition of *The New York Review of Books* on the amazing life and times of Chang and Eng Bunker, the iconic 19th century conjoined twins.

Theirs is an incredible life-story: Born in 1811 on a houseboat in Siam (now Thailand), and connected at the sternum with their livers fused, they would become history's most famous conjoined siblings – the first Siamese twins. They died in 1874 in North Carolina, but not before marrying sisters, siring 21 offspring and quasi-illegally obtaining US citizenship.

The twins were exploited by being put on display on the growing human 'freak show' circuit. Saidy notes that both reviews make much play of their chess skills, and he writes: 'Chess-playing had been one of the stunts of these conjoined twins at first public display at age 18 in Boston in 1829... and it begs the question, how did they learn western chess, since the Thai

and Chinese varieties were surely prevalent in the childhood of Chang & Eng?'

And indeed the inseparable siblings did play western chess from an early age and right throughout their lives. In 1870, they even made newspaper headlines when Chang suffered a near-fatal stroke at the board while they were playing against the president of Liberia on a steamship.

But we think we have an answer for Dr. Saidy. The first westerner to 'discover' and exploit the conjoined siblings was Robert Hunter, a Scottish businessman who lived in Siam (then a British colonial state). He took ownership of the twins when they were aged just 13 and brought them to the west to make money from them as sideshow exhibits. Being an educated Scot, it's a reasonable assumption that he taught them to play chess as part of their schtick. And indeed, in one of

An etching of Robert Hunter playing western chess with Siamese twins Chang and Eng.

the early publicity etchings of Chang and Eng, they are seen playing chess with their Scottish owner.

## Karpov Not Kasparov

Move over Juga, there's a new chess-themed boy band in town! The latest on the gig scene that has come to our attention is the Bucharest combo Karpov Not Kasparov – a band who have been quietly gaining a name for themselves across mainland Europe. According to one music critic, their 80's dance-floor sounds 'produce goosebump-inducing elec-

tronic pop music with a flair which reflects their multi-ethnic Romanian roots'.

The duo, Valerius Borcos and Eduard Gabia, are tipped as being one of Eastern Europe's best music exports for the future. The boys began making music based on the rules and strategies of chess, and so far their output is limited to a few EPs – the first track, 'Mechanical Turk', released in 2011 – and their debut album, 'Soundtrack To A Game Of Chess' (on the Berlin label, PolychromeSounds), that was nominated 'album of the month' by Vice Magazine on its release. At the moment they are busy working on the 'notoriously difficult', follow-up second album.

Apart from the chess-inspired name, albums and tracks, during live performances the chess-loving musicians also often project live tournament games as they play (hopefully while not infringing any World Chess/Agon live broadcast rights!). In a recent interview, they also revealed that one of the songs from their new album is named after Bobby Fischer's last words: 'Nothing Is As Healing As The Human Touch'.

But how did they pick their name? Well, explains Borcos: 'When we realized that our process of making music is very similar to playing chess, the next thing that came in mind were these two Russian players: Karpov and Kasparov. The irony is we prefer Kasparov to Karpov.' ∎

# NEW IN CHESS bestsellers

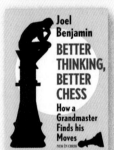
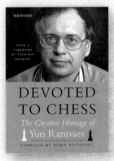
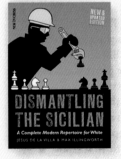
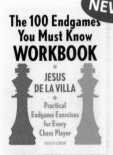

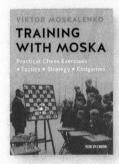

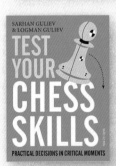

## William Lombardy

Your excellent piece on GM William Lombardy in New In Chess 2019/3, 'The Ties that Bind' by Joe Ponterotto, prompts me to share my personal reflection from long ago. In 1990, while playing in an Under-2000 tournament at the Marshall Chess Club in New York, a man sat down next to me and watched the ending of a game I was playing. When the game was over he commended me on the trap I used to win. He asked if I could show him the entire game and I obliged. It was an unusual request from a bystander, but I assumed he was a beginner and interested in learning. I was feeling good about myself for winning and was happy to further this guy's chess education. Before beginning, I wanted to have a good idea how to frame the 'lesson', so I

## 'I asked my new student what he was rated. "About 2500", was his matter-of-fact reply.'

asked my new student what he was rated. 'About 2500', was his matter-of-fact reply. Slightly embarrassed now, I asked, 'Who are you?' and he replied, 'William Lombardy.'

Needless to say, the 'teacher' quickly became the student and instead of giving a lesson to a chess legend I kindly received one!

Jay Kleinman
Franklin Square, NY, USA

## Good foresight

I would like to contribute a quote of mine for your Fair & Square column. It's a kind of prophecy, that you might find valuable enough to reach your readers. 'You could say a new era of chess has begun in Norway

and in the Nordic countries for that matter. This is only the new beginning, and you will find much more of it, and yourself in it, in the time to come!' I said this in my welcoming words, in my capacity (then) of Pres-

**Write to us**
New In Chess, P.O. Box 1093
1810 KB Alkmaar, The Netherlands
or e-mail: editors@newinchess.com
Letters may be edited or abridged

ident of the Nordic Chess Federation and chief arbiter at the 2001 Bergen Chess International/Nordic Chess Championship, where a 10-year-old chess prodigy drew against a GM for the first time. The name of the chess prodigy was Magnus Carlsen.

Arild Rimestad
Copenhagen, Denmark

## Sammy Reshevsky

Can I commend Bruce Monson on his excellent article on Sammy Reshevsky in New In Chess 2019/1. The article was well researched and also sheds light on Reshevsky's character. 'Battling' would be a generous interpretation for a little boy – and man – who it would seem had little consideration for ethics. After years of being the centre of attraction in the US Chess world, it must have irked Reshevsky to be relegated to a secondary position by Bobby Fischer.

The article brings out some interesting points – the incontrovertible evidence of 1909 as his birth year, Reshevsky having played almost every World Champion since Emanuel Lasker (and beating many of them), and his impressive US Championship record. Reuben Fine, another great player, did not win it even once.

Many decades ago, in 1980 I think it was, I was visiting a chess club in New York and remember watching

a slightly-built elderly person with a toupee, fidgety and quick, playing some blitz games. It was Reshevsky.

Srihari Iyengar
United Kingdom

## Nakamura at Gibraltar

In your article on the Gibraltar Chess Festival in New In Chess 2019/2 I couldn't help but notice the sentence 'It was in 2015 that Hikaru Nakamura decided to play here for the first time...' I played there in 2007 and Hikaru was playing as well, as a quick online search will verify.

Dale Sharp
Peekskill, NY USA

## Editorial postscript

Of course you are right, this was a typo. Hikaru Nakamura made his debut in Gibraltar ten years earlier, in 2005. He also played there in 2007, 2008 and 2009, skipped the editions 2010-2014 (playing in Wijk aan Zee) and returned to the Rock in 2015 to win the event three times in a row.

### COLOPHON

PUBLISHER: Allard Hoogland
EDITOR-IN-CHIEF:
Dirk Jan ten Geuzendam
HONORARY EDITOR: Jan Timman
CONTRIBUTING EDITOR: Anish Giri
EDITORS: Peter Boel, René Olthof
PRODUCTION: Joop de Groot
TRANSLATORS: Ken Neat, Piet Verhagen
SALES AND ADVERTISING: Remmelt Otten

PHOTOS AND ILLUSTRATIONS IN THIS ISSUE:
Alina l'Ami, Maria Emelianova, Lars O.A.
Hedlund, Lennart Ootes, Eric van Reem

COVER PHOTO: Maria Emelianova

© No part of this magazine may be reproduced,
stored in a retrieval system or transmitted in any
form or by any means, recording or otherwise,
without the prior permission of the publisher.

NEW IN CHESS
P.O. BOX 1093
1810 KB ALKMAAR
THE NETHERLANDS

PHONE: 00-31-(0)72-51 27 137
SUBSCRIPTIONS: nic@newinchess.com
EDITORS: editors@newinchess.com
ADVERTISING: otten@newinchess.com

WWW.NEWINCHESS.COM

**Magnus Carlsen has the world in awe again**

# The Emperor Strikes Back

Those who were daydreaming that the gap between Magnus Carlsen and his closest rivals was closing, are wide awake again. With phenomenal victories in the Vugar Gashimov Memorial and the Grenke Classic the World Champion demonstrated that he continues to be in a class of his own. According to **DIRK JAN TEN GEUZENDAM** the fresh energy and joyful creativity of the Norwegian's play begs to be savoured and admired, and his chances of breaking the 'unattainable' 2900 mark look more realistic than ever.

We have become accustomed to it, but let's not forget that only a short while ago it was quite different. When 'professional draws' were not frowned upon and there seemed nothing wrong with two top players ignoring a board full of pieces and prematurely splitting the point with a nod of mutual understanding – a time when, come the first time-control, several professionals believed they had tried hard enough and the stage was half-empty or simply deserted before you knew it.

looks for his chances and asks questions. Deep questions, trivial questions and often questions that make you wonder what they are all about. With endless patience. You might call it stubbornness, you might also call it love for the game. Hoping to find something he didn't yet know, something that may help him win the game. The endless inquisitiveness that marks the greatest players.

Making perseverance and endless fighting spirit your trademark also has a downside. You look less impressive when you are not in your best

it were those lean spells that encouraged his rivals. Only months ago, his total domination in the world rankings seemed to be slowly chipped away, and the magic seemed to have vanished, with his endless grinds becoming less and less successful.

But look at Magnus Carlsen now, after three major classical victories in 2019 in Wijk aan Zee, in Shamkir and in Karlsruhe/Baden-Baden. With fresh and imaginative play he dazzled his fans and, not important for a player so harshly critical of himself, he managed a happy smile to his face. In those three tournaments, Carlsen gained 40 rating points, which propelled him to 2875.4, only 13.8 points shy of his all-time high of 2889.2, which he reached five years ago, in April 2014. The gap between the world's number one and runner-up Fabiano Caruana, which was a mere 3(!) points last December, is now a telling 56.7 points again.

## Magnus Carlsen plays on because he feels that he is better than his opponent and he has a deep urge to prove it.

Those days are largely behind us, thanks to new rules requiring some minimal effort, bans on draw offers and, most importantly, inspiring trail-blazers (just fill in the names of your favourite players) that didn't need such exhortations.

And, of course, you need the reigning World Champion as a leading light. That's what I thought when I was watching Magnus Carlsen on stage at the Grenke Classic, deeply immersed in an endgame. Working late at the office when most colleagues have gone home, but there's still work to be done. On many nights recently, Carlsen worked overtime, and he was generously rewarded for his efforts.

### Always asking questions
Over the years, Carlsen has taken 'playing on' to a new level. He always plays on, it's as simple as that, unless there is an extraordinary situation, e.g. Game 12 of the London title match, when entirely different considerations were at issue. He plays on because he feels that he is better than his opponent and he has a deep urge to prove it. Even in positions in which others would start yawning, he

form. Suddenly you are not working miracles by finding an incredible twist in a position that looked bloodless, but your prolonged pushing is going nowhere and you are only hitting your head against a brick wall. It has happened to Carlsen, and

### Inevitable speculation
Form is a fickle mistress, but when the best player in the world suddenly regains his old lustre and bedaz-

MARIA EMELIANOVA

**Swarmed by fans hoping for selfies and autographs after each game, Magnus Carlsen remains easily the most popular chess player wherever the World Champion plays.**

## On his way to 2900?

Magnus Carlsen's recent successes have rekindled the expectation that the World Champion might be the first player ever to reach (and cross) the magic 2900 mark. Going by his 2900+ performances so far, these hopes do not seem unrealistic.

Below is an overview of all his 2900+ performances in tournaments with at least 8 rounds as collected by Norwegian chess journalist Tarjei Svensen. Not included are his wins in the 2013 Sinquefield Cup (4½/6 with a 2986 performance) and the 2014 Zurich Chess Challenge (4/5 with a 3026 performance).

|  | Score | TPR |
|---|---|---|
| Nanjing 2009 | 8/10 | 3002 |
| London 2012 | 6½/8 | 2990 |
| Shamkir 2019 | 7/9 | 2990 |
| Karlsruhe/Baden-Baden 2019 | 7½/9 | 2984 |
| Shamkir 2015 | 7/9 | 2984 |
| Wijk aan Zee 2013 | 10/13 | 2932 |
| Bazna 2010 | 7½/10 | 2920 |
| Nanjing 2010 | 7/10 | 2903 |
| Isle of Man | 7½/9 | 2902 |

zles everyone with his play again, it is hard not to look for explanations. From his own words it is clear that the World Championship match in London played an important role. Due to the immense pressure it was a competition he didn't really enjoy, and there was an immense feeling of liberation when the match was behind him and he had preserved his title and the number one position in the FIDE rankings. But the match also left him with an abundance of unused opening preparation that served him well in the ensuing tournaments and will no doubt continue to be valuable in the next events he will play in.

A further factor is mentioned by Jan Timman, whose column in this issue is exclusively dedicated to the recent successes of Carlsen. Timman points at the inspiration that Carlsen must have derived from *Game Changer*, the book that Matthew Sadler and Natasha Regan wrote about AlphaZero. Like all great champions, Carlsen plays a leading role in following the latest trends, and this inevitably includes the new light that is shone on our game, not only by AlphaZero but also by the latest version of Stockfish, as could be gleaned from his opening preparation for the London match.

And finally, the official reporter of the Grenke Classic ventured an explanation when, in his final interview with the winner, he cautiously wondered if perhaps there was something in his private life that made him play so well – a daring gambit, since Carlsen is generally very protective of his private life. A clear exception was the 2017 Isle of Man tournament, where he openly shared his happiness about his fine result there with his then girlfriend in front of many cameras. That relationship came to an end, and when he was asked about possible female support on the eve of the London match, he bluntly quipped: 'Women hate me, I repel them.' This was generally interpreted as a joke, even though he sounded like a man whose emotions had been hurt. When he was quizzed on the same subject in Shamkir, Carlsen deftly shut it down by saying that he had not thought about marriage yet and that he was married with chess. In Baden-Baden, he was less dismissive and replied to the interviewer's suggestive question with a broad grin and the words: 'I just feel good in general.'

And that's certainly what his recent games feels like – the accomplishments of a champion who feels good in general. In this and Jan Timman's article, you will find highlights from Magnus Carlsen's victories in Shamkir and the Grenke Classic. If you feel that our spotlights are entirely on the winner and that the other participants are being crudely neglected, you are right, and we apologize, but such was the World Champion's supremacy that we wanted to show you as much of it as possible.

## Shamkir

Magnus Carlsen has been a regular participant in the tournament that honours the memory of Vugar Gashimov, the brilliant Azeri grandmaster who tragically died in 2014 at the age of 27. This was the fourth time he took part, and as if to prove once again how much he feels at home in Shamkir, he took first place for the fourth time. But never before was he so much stronger than the rest, finishing a full two points ahead of runners-up Ding Liren and Alexander Grischuk.

Carlsen left a deep impression by winning his final three games. His dashing win in Round 7 against Anish Giri can be found in Jan Timman's column. Carlsen's second, Peter Heine Nielsen, lets you relive his amazing final two wins against Sergey Karjakin and Alexander Grischuk.

NOTES BY
**Peter Heine Nielsen**

**Sergey Karjakin**
**Magnus Carlsen**
Shamkir 2019 (8)
Sicilian Defence, Sveshnikov Variation

### 1.e4 c5!?

In view of the tournament standings, this was maybe a somewhat surprising move. Magnus was leading the tournament half a point ahead of Karjakin, who in his turn was a full point ahead of the rest of the field. For Karjakin this meant that he was basically in a 'must-win' situation: if this game was drawn, he would need, not only to score half a point more in the final round, but also to win a playoff. Even so, Magnus stayed loyal to the Sveshnikov, which generally does promise solidity but, as we saw in the London World Championship match, also allows White to set up a very complex battle.

**2.♘f3 ♘c6 3.d4 cxd4 4.♘xd4 ♘f6**

**5.♘c3 e5 6.♘db5 d6 7.♘d5!?**

Karjakin picks up the gauntlet and follows in Caruana's footsteps. After London, Magnus had won as Black against Van Foreest in Wijk aan Zee and also beaten Navara in this line earlier on in Shamkir. Magnus said afterwards that he was indeed happy to see 7.♘d5 on the board, because it always leads to very exciting positions, and while the engines seem to prefer White, Black's position is easier to play, and people tend to underestimate the human factor. Black is generally gunning for the enemy king, while White has to balance positional gains on the queenside with minding the security of his king.

**7...♘xd5 8.exd5**

**8...♘e7!?**
The move from Game 12 of the match and the tiebreak, and the one that

Sergey Karjakin challenged Magnus Carlsen in the Sveshnikov that has served the World Champion so well in the past months. It was a sobering experience for the Russian.

he also played against Van Foreest. 8...♘b8 is of equal value, as we saw in Games 8 and 10, and in the game against Navara. Karjakin couldn't possibly know which move to expect.
**9.c4 ♘g6 10.♕a4 ♗d7 11.♕b4**

**11...♗f5**
The move from Game 12. Later on Magnus preferred 11...♕b8. Anyway,

this is very much a theoretical debate in progress, in which the status of the choices is very much unsettled. Actually, it is rare at top level these days that a popular opening variation suddenly contains an oasis of almost untouched yet very interesting positions.
**12.♕a4 ♗d7 13.♕b4 ♗f5 14.h4 h5**

**15.♗g5!?**
Karjakin, of course, has come prepared and plays the critical move. Caruana went 15.♗e3, but got into trouble before the game controversially ended in a sudden draw (when Carlsen offered a draw and went for

## 'It is rare at top level these days that a popular opening variation suddenly contains an oasis of almost untouched yet very interesting positions.'

the tiebreak in the final position of Game 12, which many people considered better for him – ed.)

**15...♛b8 16.♗e2 a6 17.♞c3**

**17...♛c7**

Only this is a novelty, since 17...♞f4 18.♗f1 ♗e7 19.♗xe7 ♚xe7 20.g3 ♞g6 21.♛b6 was played in a game between Houdini and Stockfish, as Grischuk pointed out in his interesting live commentary during Game 12 of the match.

Magnus's idea, however, is very different and much more human. He does not want to leave his king vulnerable in the centre. On the contrary, it will be hidden safely away before he launches an attack on the enemy king. That the price is the h5-pawn is of no significance. Black is playing for mate!

**18.g3 ♗e7 19.♗e3 e4!**

This is the key point. Of course, ...♞f8-d7 and covering h5 before castling is also possible, but this is so much more tempting, because the knight on e5 touches the vital squares f3 and d3, and starts making White's 'aggressive' moves h4 and g3 look like weaknesses.

**20.0-0 0-0 21.♗xh5 ♞e5 22.♗e2 ♛d7**

White has won a pawn, but Black immediately zooms in on the sore spots in White's position, threatening 23...♗g4, followed by a deadly invasion on the f3-square.

**23.♛a4 ♛c8!**

Obviously not allowing a queen swap, while still maintaining the threat of ...♗g4, meaning that Karjakin has to do something.

**24.c5?!**

This is too ambitious, and tips the game in Black's favour. 24.♛d1! was the right move, controlling g4.

Indeed, Black is perfectly fine after 24...♞xc4, when 25.♗xc4 ♛xc4 26.♗d4 leads to an equal position. That was, however, the best White's position had on offer, as now things only get worse. Much worse.

**24...dxc5 25.♞xe4**

**25...c4!?** After the game Magnus was happy with this move. 25...b5 was also possible, forcing White to 'self-pin' with 26.♛c2. But, as the computer shows, after 25...c4 26.♛c2! is still the best move, so why 'force' White in the right direction?

**26.♞c3**

**26...b5!**

| Shamkir 2019 | | | | 1 | 2 | 3 | 4 | 5 | 6 | 7 | 8 | 9 | 10 | | cat. XXII |
|---|---|---|---|---|---|---|---|---|---|---|---|---|---|---|---|
| | | | | | | | | | | | | | | | TPR |
| 1 Magnus Carlsen | IGM | NOR | 2845 | * | ½ | 1 | ½ | 1 | 1 | ½ | 1 | ½ | 1 | 7 | 2990 |
| 2 Ding Liren | IGM | CHN | 2812 | ½ | * | ½ | ½ | 1 | ½ | 1 | 0 | ½ | ½ | 5 | 2817 |
| 3 Sergey Karjakin | IGM | RUS | 2753 | 0 | ½ | * | ½ | ½ | 1 | ½ | ½ | ½ | 1 | 5 | 2824 |
| 4 Teimour Radjabov | IGM | AZE | 2756 | ½ | ½ | ½ | * | ½ | ½ | ½ | ½ | ½ | ½ | 4½ | 2780 |
| 5 Alexander Grischuk | IGM | RUS | 2771 | 0 | 0 | ½ | ½ | * | ½ | 1 | 1 | ½ | ½ | 4½ | 2779 |
| 6 Viswanathan Anand | IGM | IND | 2779 | 0 | ½ | 0 | ½ | ½ | * | ½ | ½ | 1 | 1 | 4½ | 2778 |
| 7 Veselin Topalov | IGM | BUL | 2740 | ½ | 0 | ½ | ½ | 0 | ½ | * | ½ | 1 | ½ | 4 | 2739 |
| 8 David Navara | IGM | CZE | 2739 | 0 | 1 | ½ | ½ | 0 | ½ | ½ | * | ½ | ½ | 4 | 2739 |
| 9 Shakhriyar Mamedyarov | IGM | AZE | 2790 | ½ | ½ | ½ | ½ | ½ | 0 | 0 | ½ | * | ½ | 3½ | 2696 |
| 10 Anish Giri | IGM | NED | 2797 | 0 | ½ | 0 | ½ | ½ | 0 | ½ | ½ | ½ | * | 3 | 2651 |

Magnus said that he had seen 26...♗d3 27.♗xd3 ♘f3+ 28.♔g2 ♘xh4+, forcing a perpetual, but while this would indeed be a good result for the tournament situation, Black's attacking options are just too tempting to pass on.

**27.♕d1 b4!**

Another power move. Sure, it ruins the solidity of Black's pawn structure, but far more importantly, it forces White's knight as far away as possible from the kingside, where the game is going to be decided. In addition, it allows Black's bishop access to the e4-square.

**28.♘a4 ♗e4 29.♕d4**

If 29.f3, then 29....♕h3! will decide.

**29...♕f5**

**30.f4?**

Logicai, but leaving Black with a winning position. Absolutely the last chance was 30.f3!, when after 30...♘xf3+ 31.♗xf3 ♗xf3 32.♕f4 White defends. Better is 30...♗xf3, but after the cool 31.♖ae1!, White is still very much in the fight. Now Magnus shows his attacking skills with a couple of powerful moves.

**30...♕g6!**

A great intermezzo. 30...♘d3 31.g4! ♕h7 32.h5 is far less clear, but by attacking g3, Black forces White to give up the protection of the f4-pawn.

**31.♗f2 ♘d3 32.h5**

**32...♕f5!**

This is the big difference, the basic point being that on 33.g4, 33...♕xf4 is now possible due to the f2-bishop blocking the f1-rook. 32...♘xf4 might look tempting, but after 33.♖ae1 ♕f5 34.♗g4!! the tables are completely turned, since 34...♕xg4 35.♖xe4 ♘e2+ 36.♔g2! is winning for White.

**33.♗g4**

Better was 33.♗xd3, but it still leads to a winning position for Black after either recapture.

**33...♕xg4 34.♖xe4 ♗d6**

# Celeb 64

John Henderson

**Rami Malek**

At this year's Oscars, Rami Malek picked up the Best Actor Award for his portrayal of Queen frontman Freddie Mercury in the biopic *Bohemian Rhapsody*. Now the sky's the limit for the Egyptian-born actor, and recently he was brought on board to play the latest Bond villain.

It's not unknown for 007 movies to feature chess, but should the producers of the yet-untitled Bond 25 require any pieces to be pushed, then they'll have no trouble in persuading Malek. He's admitted in interviews he enjoys chess and it played a major part in his breakthrough role as computer hacker Elliot Alderson in the USA Network television series *Mr. Robot*.

Chess became a revolving theme in Season 2 of the cult series, with Malek's character involved in four games against his dark side, Mr. Robot (Christian Slater). Both actors admitted to having so much fun while filming all those key chess scenes. There was a Lasker quote, and the first three games ended in the unlikely scenario of stalemates; one of them being the shortest known stalemate, composed by Sam Loyd, another the shortest double stalemate by Enzo Minerva. Many chess-heads were confused by this, but you really needed to be a big fan of the show to get it: all the other characters, save for Elliot, are imagined, everything in his world is a creation; it's just a chess game Elliot is playing against himself, in his mind. ■

Threatening to take on f4, of course. This can be prevented, but the main theme is that Black's d3-knight is controlling the e1-square, so that his rooks can penetrate along the e-file unopposed.

**35.♕g2 ♖ae8! 36.♗d4**

**36...♕xh5!**

Precision to the end. 36...♖e2 37.♕f3! would force a queen swap, leaving White with some hope in quite a bad endgame. Now, however, 37...♖e2 is a deadly threat, since the subsequent 38.♕f3 would allow mate on h2.

**37.♕f3 ♕g6!**

Again seemingly slow, but, as on move 34, Black uses the threat to the f4-pawn to gain time for his real aims.

**38.♔h1 ♖e4! 39.♗f2 ♖fe8**

Black's threats are legion: 40...♘xf4, 40...♖e2 or 40...♘xf2+, followed by 41...♖e3. Karjakin had seen enough and resigned.

And so Magnus won the Shamkir tournament with a round to spare, but also scored his 4th(!) win in a row against 7.♘d5. Similarities to Kasparov's tournament dominance and his King's Indian come to mind.

NOTES BY
**Peter Heine Nielsen**

**Magnus Carlsen
Alexander Grischuk**
Shamkir 2019 (9)
Ruy Lopez, Berlin Defence

**1.e4 e5 2.♘f3 ♘c6 3.♗b5 ♘f6**

Since he was trailing Magnus by 1½ points, Alexander Grischuk had to focus on the fight for second place which, before going into the final round, he was sharing with Ding Liren and Sergey Karjakin. As a result, he chose the Berlin's solidity over the Najdorf's aggressiveness.

**4.d3 ♗c5 5.c3**

**5...0-0** Earlier in the tournament, Grischuk had played the popular 5...d5 against Vishy Anand, but now he reverts to the main line.

**6.0-0 d6 7.♗a4!?**

A move that is by itself enough to explain the popularity of the Berlin. If White is going to play ♗a4 anyway, then 3...a6 must really be a bad move! More seriously, this is the

kind of position in which White will make 'half moves' like 7.h3 or 7.♖e1, anyway, meaning that ♗a4 cannot be that much worse than a waiting move. Still, it does look odd!

**7...♘e7 8.♗c2 ♘g6 9.d4 ♗b6 10.a4!?**

Apart from the obvious threat of 11.a5, winning a piece, White's general concept is that he will push his a-pawn as far forward as possible, then create confusion on the other side of the board, and use this to queen his a-pawn. If that sounds like a fairy-tale, then have a look at the remainder of the game!

**10...c6 11.dxe5!?**

Very simplistic. White has just secured an advantage in the centre, but immediately gives it up, creating a symmetrical structure only for the sake of being able to push the a-pawn.

**11...♘xe5** Going by logic, Black does very little wrong in this game, except maybe for this. He exchanges a knight that has spent several tempi to relocate to g6 for a white counter-part that had moved only once.

**12.♘xe5 dxe5 13.♕xd8 ♖xd8 14.a5** For what it's worth, Magnus has achieved his aim.

**14...♗c5**

The active choice. 14...♗c7 is obviously more passive, but it does contain an important idea: after 15.♗e3 ♗e6 16.f3 b6!? Black forces White into a decision on the queenside: 17.a6!? is obviously the critical move, but since Black has not played ...b5, it means that a7 is not a target and that it is very unclear whether White's a6-pawn is a weakness or an asset. Of course, 17.axb6 is possible, but then Black's operation has been a success in the sense that White's queenside pressure has evaporated.

**15.♘d2 ♗e6**

**16.♖e1**

Since Black could meet 16.♘b3 with 16...♘xe4!, White must consolidate before continuing with his plan. Now 16...♘d7 17.♘b3 ♗e7 is possible, but after 18.♗e3 White seems to have a slight edge due to the vulnerability of Black's queenside structure. Black has been playing solidly and logically so far, so why should Grischuk start making concessions now?

**16...b5!?**

Grabbing space and potentially threatening ...a6, when Black might even start claiming that White's pawn is a weakness. White, on the other hand, is not that thrilled about pushing a6 himself too early, since it would open the b6-square for Black's bishop.

**17.♘b3**

Alexander Grischuk seemed to get a satisfactory position out of the opening and his subsequent play also looked logical and healthy, but that was not enough against Magnus Carlsen.

**17...♗xb3**

Obviously a debatable move, but also typical of Grischuk's 'high-level' style. Not restricting himself to general considerations like 'White now has the bishop pair', Grischuk goes further, saying, yes, White of course gets the bishop pair, but in return I get control of the d-file and avoid the otherwise moderately awkward pressure against my queenside. At the same time, my minor pieces are activated, while White's

bishop pair will struggle to find natural squares to develop to.

However, 17...♘d7!? might have been the better way: 18.♘xc5 ♘xc5 19.♗e3 ♗b3! forces an interesting opposite-coloured bishops position after 20.♗xc5 ♗xc2 21.a6. The human perspective is that Black's a7-pawn will be a perpetual weakness, and rook exchanges will not magnify that problem. However, Black can argue that, since he controls the d-file, White has no way to make progress. Black will just double his rooks on d7 and d8, solidly covering the a7-pawn, basically with an impregnable fortress – at least if the engines are to be believed.

**18.♗xb3 ♘g4**

Active, but not really creating more than an easily parried threat. 18...♖ab8!? 19.♔f1 b4 means that both black rooks will be controlling the open files, but after 20.♗a4!? White restricts Black's immediate activity, while at the same time attacking his weaknesses.

**19.♖e2 ♖d6** Creating the threat of 20...♘xf2 21.♖xf2 ♖f6!.

# 'If that sounds like a fairy-tale, then have a look at the remainder of the game!'

**Jonathan Rowson**: 'The game was a kind of mirror for my own mind, in which I got to understand myself better, and became very interested in my mistakes. That's what kept me in chess: a fascination with how our mind can screw up.' *(Interviewed for Emerge, the philosophical media platform, on how chess became a gateway to exploring how spirituality can be harnessed to tackle the world's interlocking environmental, political and social crises)*

**Peter Svidler**: 'In order to avoid playing the opening theory, you need to study a lot of opening theory.'

**Imad Khachan**: 'Anybody who doesn't speak any language can sit here and play chess and hold a meaningful conversation without a single word.' *(The owner of the Chess Forum, the last remaining chess shop/cafe in New York City, which was the subject of a recent short documentary film, King of the Night, from filmmakers Molly Brass and Stephen Tyler)*

**Ashot Nadanian**: 'Learn from each one of your defeats; your losses must be as close to you as victories.' *(The Armenian IM and chess coach, writing in the Singapore Chess News, November 2010)*

**Maxime Vachier-Lagrave**: 'Perfect mastery is a trap. It's a fiction, a fantasy, even a madness.

The chess player must realize that it doesn't exist. But he must act as if it does, and do his utmost to come close to it.' *(In his recent chess autobiography, Joueur d'échecs)*

**H. G. Wells**: 'Compulsory quick moving is the thing for gaiety, and that is why, though we revere Steinitz and Lasker, it is Bird we love.' *(In the chess-loving famous author's 1897 collection of essays, Certain Personal Matters)*

**C.H.O'D Alexander**: 'Alas, barely a tempo.' *(In reply to a French interviewer, when asked 'Does this make you a Knight?' after the two-time British champion and Enigma codebreaker was awarded the top honour of the Order of St. Michael and St. George by the Queen)*

**Maurice Ashley**: 'You playing chess well is just a reflection of your inner thought process and your ability to maintain discipline throughout... If we can teach every child that, then we've taught them to be better people, better friends, and better citizens.'

**David Bronstein**: 'When everything on the board is clear it can be so difficult to conceal your thoughts from your opponent.'

**Peter Hammill**: 'No more rushing around, no more travelling chess; /I guess I'd better sit down, you know I do need the rest..../Yes, it's time to

resign with equanimity and placidity /From the game.' *(The lyrics to In the End, from the chess-mad lead singer-songwriter of English prog-rock group Van Der Graaf Generator fame, on his 1973 second solo album, Chameleon in the Shadow of the Night)*

**Steve Carell**: 'I look at improvising as a prolonged game of chess. There's an opening gambit with your pawn in a complex game I have with one character, and lots of side games with other characters, and another game with myself – and in each game you make all these tiny, tiny moves that get you to the endgame.' *(In The New Yorker magazine June 2010 profile of the American comedian and Hollywood actor)*

**George Orwell**: 'He examined the chess problem and set out the pieces. It was a tricky ending, involving a couple of knights. "White to play and mate in two moves." Winston looked up at the portrait of Big Brother. White always mates, he thought with a sort of cloudy mysticism. Always, without exception, it is so arranged. In no chess problem since the beginning of the world has black ever won. Did it not symbolise the eternal, unvarying triumph of Good over Evil? The huge face gazed back at him, full of calm power. White always mates.' *(From the author's dystopian novel, 1984)*

**20.♗g5 ♔f8 21.♖f1!**

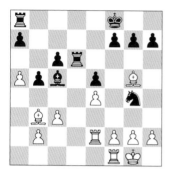

By putting pressure on f2, Grischuk might have forced this 'passive' move, but only the first part of this conclusion is actually true. White indeed had no choice but to put his rook on f1, but he does so happily, since it fits in very well with the next part of his expansion plans.

**21...♘f6 22.g3!**

Another beautiful move combining the necessary with the useful. With f4 potentially being White's way to progress, removing his king from the pin on the g1-a7 diagonal is mandatory. This also adds the option of recapturing with the g-pawn on f4, and opens a route towards the centre for White's king via g2 and later f3.

**22...a6 23.♔g2 ♘d7 24.♗c1!**

Answering the question of which square White should develop his bishop to. The key part was getting his a1-rook into play, and with that accomplished, White's dark-squared bishop happily returns to its original square, where it is safely 'out of the way', while still ready to join the battle at any given time.

**24...♗a7 25.f4 f6 26.h4!**

I first met Magnus when giving a guest-lecture at a youth camp for the youngest group of Norwegian talents, back in 2002. I spoke of Larsen, and obviously had a set of exercises in which the correct answer was always: push the h-pawn! Natasha Regan's and Matthew Sadler's fascinating book *Game Changer* devotes a full chapter to AlphaZero's preference – compared to other engines – to aggressively push its flank pawns. It would have warmed the Danish giant's heart to know that a theme he had consistently described as being underestimated in chess, is now being confirmed and refined by cutting-edge technology. If a5 and h5 look odd to you in this game, just think of the importance of having the black weak pawn at a6, and access to g6 for White's bishop. It's those details that make Black's position collapse,

> ## 'Grischuk said that this move looked like counterplay to him, but Magnus' next move was a cold shower.'

and they are created precisely by the advance of White's flank pawns.

**26...♖e8 27.h5 h6 28.♗a2 c5**

With hindsight, this is a move that is very easy to criticize, but as Grischuk pointed out at the press-conference, this is exactly what it is: with hindsight. To him it looked like it was the perfect timing, because White still seemed to need a move to consolidate before taking aggressive measures, due to the weakness of the e4-pawn.

Since that premise turns out to be wrong, Black's best bet would have been to seek counterplay with 28...exf4 29.gxf4 ♘c5, the idea being 30.e5 ♘d3!, when Black still is in the game.

**29.♗e3!**

An easy move to miss, as it indeed sacrifices a full central pawn. 29.c4 is the alternative given by the computers which, funnily enough, simultaneously blocks Black's a7-bishop and White's a2-one! White is better, but in a much less spectacular way than in the game.

**29...exf4 30.gxf4 ♖xe4 31.♗b1 ♖e7 32.♖fe1**

White has given away a full pawn, but has the threat of 33.♗g6, when 34.♗xc5 becomes deadly due to mating motifs on the e8-square.

**32...f5?**

The surprising 32...♘b8! was the correct way to fight on, in hopes of being able to follow up with ...♘c6, ...♖dd7 and ...c4. Obviously, White will forcefully prevent this liberation attempt with 33.♔f3 ♘c6 34.♗f5!?, stopping the rook from reaching d7, and meeting 34...c4? with 35.♗xa7 ♖xe2 36.♖xe2 ♘xa7 37.♗g6! ♖d8 38.♖e6!, picking up the pawn on a6 and winning easily.

**33.♗xf5 ♘f6 34.♔f3 ♘d5**

Grischuk said that this move looked like counterplay to him, but Magnus' next move was a cold shower.

**35.罝d2!** White was better anyway, but, as so often in favourable positions, the tactics also work in his favour. 35...②xe3 36.罝xd6 ②xf5 37.罝xe7 is just winning for White, as the rook and the passed pawn easily outmanoeuvre Black's two minor pieces: 37...②xe7 38.罝xa6 皇b8 39.罝a8! ②c6 40.a6, followed by 41.罝xb8 ②xb8 42.a7 being a sample line.

35...皇b8 was a line the players both looked at, but rejected in view of 36.皇xc5! 罝xe1 37.罝xd5, when 37...當e7 is met by the pretty 38.罝e5+!, and after 38...罝xe5 39.fxe5 White ends up with an extra piece.

**35...罝d8 36.皇e4 罝ed7 37.罝ed1**

No tactical magic is needed anymore.

Despite being nominally a pawn down, White aims for general exchanges!

**37...②f6 38.罝xd7 ②xd7**

Maybe 38...罝xd7 was more illustrative, as after 39.罝xd7 ②xd7 40.皇b7 ②b8 41.當e4 Black's bishop is completely

## To quote Grischuk himself: 'Magnus played incredibly well.'

tied up, because the knight needs to block its only available square in order to defend the pawn on a6.

**39.罝d6!**

And here Grischuk resigned. White will win the a-pawn and then mechanically queen after 罝xa6 皇b8 罝a8, followed by a6 and a7.

In many ways an amazing game. White got nothing out of the opening, and Black's moves from there on all looked healthy and logical. To quote Grischuk himself: 'Magnus played incredibly well.'

■ ■ ■

## Grenke Classic

Only 10 days separated the Gashimov Memorial from the Grenke Classic, but that barely seemed to affect Magnus Carlsen, who continued where he left off and started with two wins. The first three rounds in Karlsruhe coincided with the final rounds of the Grenke Open, an immense gathering of chess players that claims to be the biggest Open in the world. And with some two thousand participants, this can hardly be called an empty boast. Literally hundreds of tables filled the main hall behind the spectator area in front of the stage of the Classic, while the remaining participants played in two other halls in the same congress building.

With two rounds a day, the first one starting at nine in the morning, the Open is no picnic, but besides many amateur players the attractive prize-fund had lured lots of grandmasters, including Etienne Bacrot, Gata Kamsky, Anton Korobov and Alireza Firouzja. The motto of the combined event is 'mass and class', as tournament director Sven Noppes explained. After you finished your game in the Open, you could watch the stars in action, including the World Champion.

Last year, the Open was sensationally won by 13-year-old Vincent Keymer. His amazing score of 8 out of 9 made him the sole winner, which added to the sensation. After all, an Open with many hundreds of participants seems to beg for a multiple tie for first. This year, the winning score was 7½, and no fewer than eight players reached that result. Again a 13-year-old was among the top-finishers,

Daniel Fridman calculated well at and away from the board. His win in the Grenke Open came with a neat paycheque and an invitation to next year's Grenke Classic.

returns. The World Champion was sharp and hungry and didn't see more deeply in only his own games. While his opponent in Round 7, Levon Aronian, was having a deep think, Carlsen spotted a neat turn in the game of Fabiano Caruana – who would finish in clear second place – against Arkady Naiditsch. Naiditsch finished third, but might have tied for second if he had seen what Carlsen saw.

**Fabiano Caruana**
**Arkadij Naiditsch**
Baden-Baden 2019 (7)

position after 17.♗f4

**17...♗c3** Naiditsch fails to spot that he can re-establish material equality with 17...♘xb3!, since 18.♘xb3 ♖d5! (as shown by Carlsen) will leave the queen with nowhere to go and White has to play 19.♘c5 (19.♕c4 ♖c8 doesn't help either) 19...♗xc5 and Black is perfectly fine.
**18.♖ac1 a6 19.♕e5 ♗xf3**
**20.♗xf3 ♗xd4 21.♕xa5 ♘d5**
**22.♗c7 ♖d7 23.e3**

Now White was a pawn up and won after 33 moves.

but India's great hope Dommaraju Gukesh had to settle for 4th place.

The winner remained unclear till the prize-giving, but there it was revealed that Daniel Fridman had won the Open. The German grandmaster struck on the penultimate day by winning both his games to become the sole leader. First he deftly defused the King's Indian of Greek GM Antonios Pavlidis and then he struck when Jorden van Foreest went astray in a position that looked fairly harmless.

**Jorden van Foreest**
**Daniel Fridman**
Karlsruhe Grenke Open 2019 (7)

position after 25...♘f7

Black's position is slightly more pleasant to play, but White should be fine.
**26.♖d3?** But this is a very unfortunate attempt to improve his position.
**26...♕e1+ 27.♔h2 ♘e5** And White resigned. He loses an exchange with absolutely no compensation.

In the last two rounds, Fridman did most of the calculating away from the board. Carefully weighing his chances he drew his final two games in 19 and 15 moves respectively, counting on the mysteries of the Buchholz system. And who could blame him? He had calculated correctly and not only took the 13,094 euro first prize but also won an invitation to next year's Classic. For the spectators, however, Buchholz and the many draws that came with it – not only in Fridman's games – felt like an unsatisfactory way to end a prestigious tournament, and hopefully the organizers will come up with something better for next year.

## Sharp and hungry
No new rules are needed for the Classic, certainly not if Magnus Carlsen

## Growing 34 centimetres

In the very first round, Magnus Carlsen faced Germany's big hope Vincent Keymer. According to the latter's trainer Peter Leko, this was a tournament purely to gain experience and to get a feeling for what this level means. Leko had advised him to play interesting positions and see how his experienced opponents dealt with them.

In the year between his win in the Open and his debut in the Classic, Keymer had grown 34 centimetres to reach an imposing 1.85 metres. He had also gained 75 rating points. His first game against the World Champion was quite an experience, and we are glad that he was prepared to share it with our readers.

NOTES BY
**Vincent Keymer**

**Vincent Keymer**
**Magnus Carlsen**
Karlsruhe 2019 (1)
Benoni Wall

Until just before the first round I had perhaps underestimated the situation at the start of the games. In the hotel I was still completely calm. But when the players were called to the stage one by one in front of a packed hall, and when I was sitting opposite the World Champion and the FIDE President made the first move, it became clearly more difficult to concentrate on my moves without being affected by the atmosphere and my emotions. And my lavish use of time in the opening can surely also partly be attributed to nervousness.

**1.d4 ♘f6 2.c4 c5 3.d5 g6 4.♘c3**

## 'My lavish use of time in the opening can surely also partly be attributed to nervousness.'

**4...d6**

4...♗g7 allows ♘h3. It is unclear if that is a problem, but in any case it's an extra option: 5.♘h3 d6 6.♘f4 0-0 7.h4!? (7.e3 doesn't look dangerous, and doesn't seem to be critical for Black either) 7...e5 8.dxe6 ♗xe6 9.♘xe6 fxe6 10.g3 ♘c6 11.♗g2, with a pleasant position for White.

**5.e4 ♗g7 6.♘f3 0-0 7.♗e2 e5 8.0-0 ♘e8 9.♘e1 f5**

**10.exf5** Not the best move, according to the engine, but practically speaking a totally normal reaction.

10.♘d3 was the right move, as Black doesn't get the hoped-for counterplay with ...f4. Black has a wide choice:

At the board, 10...f4 was my only reason not to play ♘d3. But after 11.a3 b6 12.b4 ♘d7 13.♗d2, White slowly attacks on the queenside, while Black can't find any real counterplay.

10...fxe4 11.♘xe4 ♘f6 12.♗g5 is a dream for White.

10...♘d7 11.a3 fxe4 is always good for White: 12.♘xe4 ♘df6 13.♘c3 ♗f5 14.♗e3. White has full control and is better thanks to his space advantage and the bad position of some of the black pieces.

10...♘f6 is the most human move: 11.exf5 gxf5 12.f3 ♘bd7 13.♘f2, with a white edge.

**10...gxf5**

**11.f4**

In this manner I wanted to steer for the structures after ...e4, which I believed would favour me.

Interesting was 11.g3!? ♘d7 12.f3, when after for instance 12...♕e7 13.♘g2 ♘c7 14.♔h1 ♔h8 15.a4 Black lacks counterplay.

**11...♘d7 12.♘d3**

Perhaps not the best. Probably White should have kept the tension, waited for Black to play ...e4 and then moved the knight to e3 anyway.

**12...e4 13.♘f2**

The knight belongs on e3! So even here White could play 13.♘e1!?.

**13...♗xc3**

This came as a surprise. I had mainly reckoned with ...♘c7 or ...a6, to push ...b5 as quickly as possible, since the present structure gives White good and pleasant play (see Jan Timman's column – p. 103 – for his comments on this move and Keymer's surprise -ed.).

So, 13...♘c7!? 14.a4 (to stop ...b5; 14.♗e3 b5 15.cxb5 a6 gives Black too much play) 14...♗d4!, with a totally unclear position that offers chances but also entails risks for both sides. Or 13...♗d4 14.♘b5, and Black has to retreat.

**14.bxc3 ♘df6**

**15.♗e3**

It was also possible to try and take the knight to e3 straightaway with 15.♕e1!?. But then White's dark-squared bishop no longer has a good square to go to. Therefore I wanted to take the bishop to f2 before transferring the knight to e3.

**15...♘g7 16.♕e1 ♗d7 17.♘d1 ♗a4** Now I have to accept either the exchange of my knight or a loss of tempo after 18.♘b2 ♗e8.

**18.h3**

**18...♗xd1** I hadn't expected this immediate capture on d1; I had counted on 18...♔h8, when I no longer have a useful move, e.g. after

Who wouldn't get nervous? As FIDE President Arkady Dvorkovich makes the first move, Vincent Keymer (14) observes Magnus Carlsen at the start of his first game against the World Champion.

the bishop is placed less than optimally with 19.♗f2. But I would probably have to play this anyway to force the capture on d1: 19...♗xd1 20.♖xd1 ♕d7 21.♗h4 ♖f7, and Black will move his other rook to g8, with an unclear position.

**19.♕xd1**

Here I had the feeling that my position should be very pleasant. The black knights have no good squares and White always has the idea of breaking the black structure with g4. 19.♗xd1!? pursues the idea to first get everything under control with ♕h4.

**19...♕e8 20.♔f2 ♕g6**

**21.♖g1**

During the game I had the feeling that 21.g4 was exactly the move Black was hoping for, and after I had seen his reply (moving the queen to h6), I relatively quickly ceased my calculations. After 21...♕h6 I had missed the resource 22.♖h1, however, but although Black now has to retreat with ...♘d7, I can hardly believe that he will not get sufficient counterplay: 22...♘d7 23.♔g1 ♘e5 24.g5 (24.♕f1 ♖ae8, with crazy complications) 24...♕g6 25.h4 ♘g4, with unclear play.

**21...♔h8**

**22.a4**

I was afraid of ...b5 if I played ♕f1 immediately.

# 'I had the feeling that my position should be winning, but didn't see exactly how.'

The position after 22.♕d2 h5 23.g3 ♖f7 I found hard to assess. In hindsight I would say that it should be about equal, even if complicated and difficult to play.

**22...♖g8 23.♕f1 ♘fh5**
After 23...h5!? 24.♔e1 h4 25.♕f2 ♕g3 26.♕xg3 hxg3 27.♖b1 ♖ab8 28.♔d2 we have reached a fortress on both sides. Neither player can do anything.

**24.g3** During the game, 24.g4 fxg4 25.hxg4 ♘xf4 looked dangerous, so no reason to calculate this further. But after 26.♗xf4 ♖af8 27.♔e3 ♕f6 28.♔d2! ♕xf4+ 29.♕xf4 ♖xf4 30.♔e3 White should be safe.

**24...♖af8 25.♕g2**
I was already under time-pressure, having only 15 minutes to get to move 40. So I tried to make logical, normal and solid-looking moves, so as not to complicate matters unnecessarily.

**25...♕f6 26.♖ac1**

**26...♕d8**
Definitely not the best. White can now go for his main idea, g4, while Black's play on the queenside is fairly slow. I think that Black decided on this move only to avoid the draw after 26...♘xg3.
But the only way to keep the balance was 26...♘xg3!! 27.♕xg3 ♘h5 28.♗xh5 ♖xg3 29.♔xg3. Luckily for me, this idea ended my moment of shock, as I didn't believe that Black could be better, never mind winning: 29...♖g8+ 30.♔h2 ♖xg1 31.♖xg1 ♕xc3 32.♖g3 ♕xc4 33.♗f7, and here Black is also risking something.
A couple of moves earlier I had planned 29.♖xg3 (instead of 29.♔xg3)

and thought that after 29...♕h4 30.♗e2 ♖g8 31.♖cg1 it should be a draw. But then I noticed that Black does have a long-term plan, viz. ...♖g7 or ...♖g6, and then transferring the king to the queenside.

**27.♕h2 ♘f6 28.g4 ♘d7 29.g5 ♕a5**
Here I again used most of my remaining time. I had the feeling that my position should be winning, but didn't see exactly how.

**30.g6?**
I had completely overlooked Black's defence on move 32. And if I don't win directly, pushing g6 robs me of any chance to ever break through. Most logical looked 30.h4, but after 30...♘b6 you'd have to see 31.♖a1

(after 31.h5 I failed to spot a direct win, which is a serious problem in time-trouble), a move that completely kills Black's counterplay, since he cannot take any of the hanging pawns: 31...♘e8 (and not 31...♕xc3? 32.♖gc1 ♕b2 33.♕g1, and the black position will slowly but surely fall apart) 32.♕h1, and the queen is brought back into play, when Black can no longer hold his position together.

**30...h6 31.♖b1**

31.♕g3 ♕d8 32.♖b1 was perhaps better than including ♖b1/...♖b8.

**31...♖b8 32.♕g3**

**32...♕d8**

White's only idea is to attack on the queenside with ♖b5, ♖gb1 and a5.

**33.♔e1?!** Again not good.

**33...♘e8**

**34.♔d2?**

I played this without much thought. Throughout the game I had wanted to take my king to safety, and now I finally got the chance. In addition, with two to three minutes on the clock you are grateful for any simple move. But unfortunately it allows Black to win my pawn on g6.

Of course, the right move was 34.h4, when after 34...♘df6 35.♔d2 ♘g7 36.h5 Black's position, with the knights on f6 and g7, should be OK.

**34...♘f8 35.♗f2**

I was hoping to somehow exchange the queens, but of course that is not permitted.

35.♗h5 only delays the loss of the pawn.

**35...♕e7**

**36.♔e3?**

I was too focused on the idea of ♕h4, without thinking of the problems it would create.

**36...♕f6** Probably even better for Black than the game was 36...♖xg6 37.♕h4 ♕g7 38.♔d2 ♘f6.

**37.♔d2**

**37...♘xg6** After 37...♖xg6 38.♕h4 (otherwise I will never have counterplay or a plan) 38...e3+ 39.♔xe3 ♕xc3+ 40.♗d3 ♘g7 41.♖gd1 Black

is of course fine, but at least White is still alive.

**38.h4 ♘e7 39.♕h3 ♖xg1 40.♖xg1 ♕f7 41.h5 ♘f6 42.♗h4 b6 43.♖b1**

I wanted to prevent my opponent exchanging rooks with ...♖g8.

**43...♕f8**

According to the engine, 43...♖g8 44.a5 bxa5 45.♖b7 ♕f8 wins for Black, but this is not the way you happily go for at the board.

**44.♖g1 ♕f7 45.♖b1 ♕g7 46.♖g1 ♕f8 47.♔c2**

After 47.♖b1 ♕f7 I didn't know what to play without making my position worse.

**47...♘fg8 48.♔d2 ♕f7 49.♔c2 ♖f8 50.♔d2 ♕e8 51.♖a1 ♖f7 52.a5 bxa5 53.♖xa5 ♘c8 54.♖a1 ♕f8 55.♖b1 ♘b6 56.♖g1**

**56...♖g7?** This gives White good drawing chances.

## 'I was too focused on the idea of ♕h4, without thinking of the problems it would create.'

Instead, 56...a5 57.♖g6 a4 wins easily; White has no threats.

**57.♖xg7 ♔xg7 58.♕g3+ ♔h8 59.♕g6 a5 60.♗f1**

60.♔c2 a4 61.♔b2 was easier.

**60...a4 61.♔c2 a3 62.♔b3 ♘a4!**

Making White's life the most difficult.

**63.♗h3**

**63...♕g7!**

A very serious try. Anything else is more or less easy for White, but this poses big practical problems.

63...a2 64.♔xa2 ♘xc3+ 65.♔b2 ♘d1+ 66.♔c1 ♘e3 67.♕g3 leads to a draw.

**64.♕xg7+ ♔xg7 65.♗xf5 ♘f6 66.♔xa3 ♘xc3**

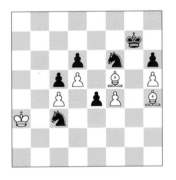

**67.♗f2??**

From here on in, White's position is hopeless.

The only way to make a draw was 67.♔b3! ♘e2 68.♗xf6+! (again the only one) 68...♔xf6 69.♗xe4 ♘xf4 70.♗f3. It's incredible, but White holds this position, even with a good black knight vs a bad white bishop, while White's h5-pawn is weak and the white pawns are on the wrong

colour: 70...♔g5 (or 70...♔e5 71.♔a4 ♔d4 72.♔b5 ♘d3 73.♗e2 ♘e5 74.♗f1, with a draw) 71.♔a4, and the white king is in time. Of course Black cannot play 71...♘xh5?? now in view of 72.♗xh5 ♔xh5 73.♔b5, and White wins.

**67...♘e2 68.♔a4 ♘xh5 69.♔a5 ♘f6 70.♔b6 ♘f7 71.♔c7 ♔e7 72.♗e3 ♘d4 73.♗g6 h5 74.♗f2 ♘f3 75.♗f5 ♘d2 76.♗h4 e3**

**77.♗d3 ♘f3 78.♗xf6+ ♔xf6 79.♔xd6 h4 80.♔c7 ♘d4 81.♔c8 e2**

White resigned.

■ ■ ■

## Bearded vs beardless

While in Shamkir Carlsen won his final three games, in the Grenke Classic he won his final four. No doubt there was no correlation, but before his game against Georg Meier in Round 6, the Norwegian had shaved off the beard he had been sporting in the early rounds. Carlsen had been worried about how he was to win that game as Black, and when he succeeded he was relieved.

The next day, he scored a smashing win against Levon Aronian, who spent tons of time in the opening and was in time-trouble from around move 20 onwards. Another explanation was given by Carlsen when he said that he finds it much easier to play against the guys he knows: 'You can just go with the flow, while with the other guys I am just over-thinking.'

The rest is explained by Anish Giri.

NOTES BY
**Anish Giri**

**Magnus Carlsen
Levon Aronian**
Baden-Baden 2019 (7)
Queen's Gambit, Vienna Variation

**1.d4 ♘f6 2.c4 e6 3.♘f3 d5 4.♘c3**

After his match against Fabiano Caruana, Magnus Carlsen is coming back to his early 1.d4 tabiya, for which he has clearly done some work.

**4...dxc4** As far as I know, Levon Aronian usually goes for the Vienna via the Ragozin move order (4...♗b4 5.♗g5 dxc4), but this is still very topical these days.

**5.e4 ♗b4**

**6.♗g5** The old main line, and in a sense already a slight surprise.

6.♗xc4 ♘xe4 7.0-0 is the variation Levon had been avoiding so far, but I guess he liked Magnus showing his hand here against Duda in Wijk aan Zee and wanted to improve on that game. There, Carlsen came up with the novelty 10.♖d1!? after 7...♘f6 8.♕a4+ ♘c6 9.♘e5 ♖b8.

**6...c5**

Levon has also been toying with the somewhat more playful 6...h6, but this is clearly his main line here.

**7.♗xc4 cxd4 8.♘xd4 ♗xc3+**

8...♕a5 is another system, in which White's established response is 9.♗d2.

**9.bxc3 ♕a5 10.♗d2**

This is a new move, which is almost weird, because all kinds of moves have been played in this position. I propose to call this beautiful variation the Magnus Carlsen Variation.

**10...0-0** I looked at the complications that arise after 10...♘xe4 and was suddenly reminded of a novelty Carlsen played in the 6. a3 e5 Najdorf against Wojtaszek in Wijk aan Zee, when he went 7.♘f5. These two ideas have a lot in common.

**11.♕e2 e5 12.♘b3 ♕c7 13.0-0 ♗g4** This idea looks very stylish, but if Levon had known that the simple 13...♖e8 would also have been met with 14.♗d5, he would probably have played that instead.

**14.f3 ♖c8 15.♗d5 ♘xd5 16.exd5 ♗h5 17.c4**

On a sofa in Shenzhen, from where we were following the game, a

Levon Aronian spent tons of time in the opening and was in time-trouble from around move 20 onwards. And then the decisive mistake was there, waiting to be made.

colleague of mine saw a 1-0 coming here. Although the prediction came a little early, the position is not easy for Black to handle. You want to do something active and push ...e4 at some point, but it is much more likely you are going to do it at the wrong moment than at the right time. White, on the other hand, has lots of easy moves at his disposal.

**17...♘d7 18.♖fc1 b6 19.a4**

**19...a5**
I don't think this push is bad structurally, but it may have been an inaccuracy because it wastes a tempo. A tempo in this position can be used for preparing some ...e4 business and, if the opportunity arises, to try and

disrupt White's regrouping, which is going to be ♕f2, ♗e3, ♕b2, ♘d2, etc., as in the game. A good way to counter this plan is the ...♕d6-♕b4 and ...♗g6-♗d3 excursions.
19...♕d6 was better anyway, because 20.a5 can be met by 20...b5! 21.cxb5 ♕xd5 22.♖xc8+ ♖xc8 23.♖c1 ♖xc1+ 24.♘xc1 e4!, with good counterplay, since the tactics work on account of the weak b5-pawn.

**20.♕f2 ♕d6 21.♗e3**

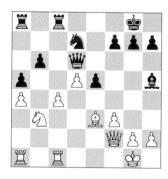

**21...♗g6**
The World Champion often pretends that he doesn't care about annoying moves like 21...♕b4!?, but deep inside they do bother him, just like they bother most players: 22.♕c2 (22.♘d2

## 'When facing a top player in good form, it is these kinds of mistakes that make a difference.'

♗g6) 22...♘f6 23.♗d2 ♕d6 24.♗g5 ♘d7 25.♗e3 ♗g6 would lead to the same position as in the game, though.

**22.♕d2**

After the game Carlsen claimed that he was hoping for 22...f6 here and didn't like that 22.♕b2 would be met by 22...♗f5 and 23...♕g6.

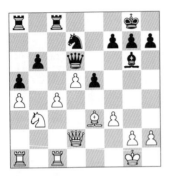

**22...f6**

22...h6!? was also possible, as c5 is not a killing threat: 23.c5 ♘xc5 24.♗xc5 bxc5 25.♘xa5 ♗d3!.

22...♗f5 would have worked as well.

**23.♕b2!**

Sending the queen to a3 looks nasty.

**23...♖c7?!**

Aimed against ♕a3, but White now starts with ♘d2.

23...♕b4! was actually a clever way to solve the little situation here: 24.♕c3 (24.♗d2 ♕d6, and the bishop occupies the square for the knight) 24...♕d6 25.♘d2 ♘c5 26.♕a3, and it's actually better for Black to have the rook on c8 rather than on c7, which becomes evident after 26...♖ab8 27.♘b3, and now the very strong 27...♕c7!.

**24.♘d2 ♘c5 25.♕a3 ♖d8 26.♖c3**

**26...f5?** When facing a top player in good form, it is these kinds of mistakes that make a difference and are unforgivable. It is easy to explain it, to call it a natural collapse under pressure, to say it was part of the general trend, not to mention the unpleasant time situation. But nothing is written in the stars, and on a good day Levon would have defended better. This is by no means a reproach, since I was actually anticipating this move, while following the game live.

After 26...♖b7!? 27.♘b3 (for example) 27...♘a6 the endgames are extremely icky for Black, but there is still a really long way to go, and the game still has to be won three times before White actually breaks through, e.g. 28.♕xd6 ♖xd6 29.♘d2 ♘b4 30.♘e4 ♖d8 31.g4 h5 32.h3 hxg4 33.hxg4 ♔f8, and this would have kept the game going.

And a similarly tight move like 26...h6 would have done the same.

**27.♖e1!**

Now there is no way for Black to avoid losing a pawn. Black has no good follow-up move, certainly not one to justify the weakening of the e5-pawn with ...f5. The only natural follow-up is swiftly refuted by White.

**27...e4 28.fxe4 fxe4 29.♗xc5 ♖xc5 30.♘xe4 ♕e5 31.♖ce3 ♖cc8** It doesn't seem so easy just yet if White tries a knight discovery, but Black actually has no threats left.

**32.h3!**

Here, as in some of my own games against Magnus, he seems to experience a sense of arousal when he spends some time in a position full of options and then makes a move like h3 or ♔h1. Then again, who doesn't?

**32...♕c7** 32...♕d4 is met by 33.♘d6!. **33.♘d2** It's over now, since White has the pawn and the compensation as well. **33...♖e8 34.♖e7 ♖xe7 35.♖xe7 ♕d8 36.♕e3 ♖c7 37.♖e6 ♖c5 38.♕b3**

And with a second pawn falling and the flag as well, Black had to admit defeat.

■ ■ ■

## A fun game

If there was still doubt about the winner, it vanished in the penultimate round, when Carlsen played what he called 'a fun game' against Peter Svidler. Everyone understood what he meant when he added: 'I don't expect to win like this every game, but the last few rounds have been just great.' And you don't very often see a top-level game finish in a neat mate.

NOTES BY
**Peter Heine Nielsen**

**Peter Svidler**
**Magnus Carlsen**
Baden-Baden 2019 (8)
Sicilian Defence, Anti-Sveshnikov Variation

**1.e4 c5 2.♘f3 ♘c6**

This has been Magnus' favourite opening of late, which he obviously played in the World Championship match, but he actually already started playing it in the 2018 Sinquefield Cup. There, Vachier-Lagrave played 3.♘c3, but since then the focus has been on first 3.♗b5 and then the popular 7.♘d5 in the Sveshnikov, in which Caruana continued his theoretical discussion with Magnus earlier in the tournament.

**3.♘c3**
Svidler copies MVL, staying away from the most principled battles.

**3...e5 4.♗c4 ♗e7!?**
In St. Louis, Magnus chose the

surprising 4...g6, but here he reverts to the standard move.

**5.d3 d6**

**6.♘d2!?** Kasparov's favourite move, aiming for the control of d5. Later, attention switched to 6.0-0 ♘f6 7.♘g5, leading to a much sharper battle. However, the positional approach has both logic and venom.

**6...♘f6** The modest 6...♗g5 was the choice in the early encounters, but modern theory has started to focus on this natural developing move.

**7.♘f1 ♘d7!?**

This has been played less, but it does follow in the footsteps of both Kramnik and Gelfand, and it was also played twice by Lenic in his 2017 World Cup match vs. Magnus' French second Laurent Fressinet.

The idea is to exchange off White's strong knight on d5, and while this could obviously also be done from f6 – so logic dictates that Black just throws away two tempi – the point is that it's done on Black's terms, trying to force White to take on b6 when the knight appears there.

**8.♘d5** 8.♘e3 was Fressinet's and Kasparov's choice, and while

White kept a nominal edge, neither managed to break down Black's solid position.

**8...♘b6 9.♘xb6!? axb6**

**10.c3** This is the point of White's play, creating a somewhat awkward double pawn, and not allowing 10.♘e3 b5!, removing the weakness due to 11.♗xb5? ♕a5+, and White loses a piece.

**10...0-0 11.♘e3 ♗g5 12.0-0**
Here Kramnik took on e3, followed by ...♕e7 and ...♗e6, equalizing. The engines have similar thoughts, suggesting 12...♗e6. But how do you actually play for a win?

**12...♔h8!?**

At least asking a question – if ...f5 next is a 'threat' – generally safeguarding the king.

Now 13.♘d5 would have been safer, since 13...♗xc1 14.♕xc1 f5 15.exf5 ♗xf5 16.♕e3 leads to a pleasant position for White, with b4 or f4 next. Svidler, however, indicates that ...f5 does not worry him, and Magnus follows up with this move, saying, 'Maybe you should be worried.'

**13.a3?! f5! 14.♘xf5 ♗xc1 15.♖xc1 ♗xf5 16.exf5 d5!**

**17.♗a2** White got bishop vs knight, but Black has the f-file and more pawns in the centre. Svidler plays ambitiously, eyeing the d5-pawn as a potential weakness, but safer would have been the liquidating 17.♗b5!?, intending 17...♖xf5 18.♗xc6, with simplification and a likely draw. Now the battle focuses around the question of whether White's bishop on a2 will be in or out of play.

**17...♖xf5 18.♕g4 ♖f6**

**19.f4?!**

The wish for exchanges, as well as annulling the pressure on the f-file, is understandable, but the ensuing tactics turn out (very) well for Black. Common sense chess with 19.♖ce1 ♕d6 20.♕d1 would bring some harmony into White's position, and while his aggressive prospects are not huge, he does have a solid position. After the game move, however, not so much.

**19...exf4 20.♕g5** A necessary intermediate move, as 20.♖xf4? loses material immediately to 20...♘e5! 21.♕g3 ♖xf4 22.♕xf4 ♘xd3.

**20...♕f8!**

While the early phase of this game of Magnus saw standard moves

combined with a bit of provocation, the remainder is a different and serious matter, since he develops a strong attack and finishes it off in style. Keeping the f4-pawn is crucial to his attacking concept, and admitting the bishop on a2 back into the game is of much lesser importance, as the continuation will show that it's shooting into thin air.

**21.♕xd5**

Rerouting the bishop to e4 with 21.♗xd5 would have been ideal strategically, but unfortunately drops a piece due to 21...♖f5!.

**21...♖d8! 22.♕f3?!**

Logical and consistent, but giving Black everything he wants.

22.♕g5 h6 23.♕h5 ♖xd3 24.♖ce1 is indeed a pawn down, but with decent compensation and good chances of a draw.

**22...♘e5 23.♕e4!?**

Svidler may have pinned his hopes on this move, hitting the knight and thus not allowing ...f3, which would be lethal after the immediate 23.♕xb7.

**23...♘g4!** Magnus is in the zone, both mentally and with the knight invading on e3, where it becomes the lynchpin of the black attack.

23...♘xd3 would leave Black a pawn up, but the attack would peter out.

**24.♖ce1 ♘e3 25.♖f2 ♖e8!**
**26.♕xb7 g5!**

First a pawn sac and then this key move as a follow-up. The knight on e3 and the pawn on f4 completely block White's rooks, and the bishop on a2 is basically on an empty diagonal, as Black's attack will happen on the dark squares. White's position might look sufficiently solid, but the march of the g-pawn drastically changes

| Karlsruhe/Baden-Baden 2019 | | | | 1 | 2 | 3 | 4 | 5 | 6 | 7 | 8 | 9 | 10 | | cat. XIX TPR |
|---|---|---|---|---|---|---|---|---|---|---|---|---|---|---|---|
| 1 Magnus Carlsen | IGM | NOR | 2845 | * | ½ | ½ | 1 | ½ | 1 | 1 | 1 | 1 | 1 | 7½ | 2983 |
| 2 Fabiano Caruana | IGM | USA | 2819 | ½ | * | 1 | ½ | ½ | ½ | ½ | ½ | 1 | 1 | 6 | 2838 |
| 3 Arkadij Naiditsch | IGM | AZE | 2695 | ½ | 0 | * | ½ | 1 | ½ | 0 | ½ | 1 | 1 | 5 | 2770 |
| 4 Maxime Vachier-Lagrave | IGM | FRA | 2773 | 0 | ½ | ½ | * | ½ | ½ | ½ | ½ | 1 | 1 | 5 | 2761 |
| 5 Vishy Anand | IGM | IND | 2774 | ½ | ½ | 0 | ½ | * | ½ | ½ | 1 | 0 | 1 | 4½ | 2718 |
| 6 Levon Aronian | IGM | ARM | 2763 | 0 | ½ | ½ | ½ | ½ | * | 1 | ½ | ½ | ½ | 4½ | 2719 |
| 7 Peter Svidler | IGM | RUS | 2735 | 0 | ½ | 1 | ½ | ½ | 0 | * | ½ | 1 | ½ | 4½ | 2722 |
| 8 Francisco Vallejo | IGM | ESP | 2693 | 0 | ½ | ½ | ½ | 0 | ½ | ½ | * | ½ | 1 | 4 | 2684 |
| 9 Georg Meier | IGM | GER | 2628 | 0 | 0 | 0 | 0 | 1 | ½ | 0 | ½ | * | 0 | 2 | 2514 |
| 10 Vincent Keymer | IM | GER | 2516 | 0 | 0 | 0 | 0 | 0 | ½ | ½ | 0 | 1 | * | 2 | 2527 |

Peter Svidler ended his game against Magnus Carlsen with a magnanimous sporting gesture, allowing a mate 'that speaks for itself in its beauty'.

this. White's position is actually so bad that there is nothing he can do, and Svidler decides to literally do that, going back and forth.

**27.♖fe2?!**
I guess this should be criticized in principle, but I cannot offer any reasonable alternative.

**27...g4 28.♖f2 ♕h6!**
Simply threatening ...g3, and then mate on h2.

**29.♕c7**
X-raying the g3-square.

**29...♖ef8!**
Renewing the threat of ...g3, with hxg3 ♘g4! now being the follow-up, as there is no longer a rook hanging on e8. White can do absolutely nothing against it.

**30.h3!?**

One might think that Svidler decided to be a good sport and allow a very spectacular finish, but actually his position is just dead lost. The computer wants tragic moves like 30.♕e5 g3 31.hxg3 ♘g4 32.♕xf6+ or 30.g3 fxg3 31.♕xg3, allowing 31...♖xf2, just to illustrate how desperate the situation is.

**30...gxh3 31.g3 fxg3 32.♖xf6!?**

The idea is that after 32...♕xf6 33.♕xg3 White fights on, but also that after **32...h2+! 33.♔h1 g2** we have a mate that speaks for itself in its beauty.

■ ■ ■

And then Carlsen won the last game, too, when Maxime Vachier-Lagrave impulsively made an opti-

mistic decision in the opening, only to discover shortly afterwards that he was simply a pawn down.

**Magnus Carlsen**
**Maxime Vachier-Lagrave**
Baden-Baden 2019 (9)

position after 10.♕d2

Here MVL went **10...b5** and White took the pawn, and after: **11.cxb5 axb5 12.♘xb5 ♕a5 13.♘c3 ♖ab8 14.♖fc1 ♖fc8 15.b3** it was hard to see Black's compensation (1-0, 43).

As Carlsen summed it up: 'It was really only one key moment, when he played ...b5, which I believe to be a completely incorrect pawn sac. So I didn't think too much. I took it and hoped for the best. And after that he is really just struggling to survive.'

And so Magnus Carlsen won his third classical tournament in 2019, dramatically improved his leading position in the world rankings and inevitably rekindled speculation about whether he can break the 2900 barrier. His own thoughts were down-to-earth: 'If you'd asked me a few weeks ago I still would have said no; that 2900 isn't possible. But now it's 25 points away. To get there I have to keep performing the way I have recently, which I very much hope to do, but it's not very realistic. But now it's at least a semi-attainable dream, which is really all I could hope for. But I don't think too much about it yet. I just want to keep going in the same way.'

Well, who wouldn't? ■

**Dutch GM wins Shenzhen Masters**

# Giri catches 'Hari' at last hurdle

A Chinese welcome for the 2019 Shenzhen Masters: Dmitry Jakovenko, Pentala Harikrishna, Richard Rapport, Anish Giri, Ding Liren and Yu Yangy

Forcefully bouncing back from an early loss, Pentala Harikrishna pulled off a four-game winning streak. The Indian ace seemed on course to win the third edition of the Shenzhen Masters until he stumbled in the last round and was overtaken by Anish Giri, exactly the man who had inflicted that early loss. **ERWIN L'AMI** travelled to China as Giri's second and reports on his friend's 'super-category' victory.

**W**ith the Grand Chess Tour having expanded in size and the new FIDE World Championship cycle taking off with multiple qualifiers, 2019 is going to be a very busy year for most of the top players. After all, in addition to these cycles there are various other elite tournaments that try to maintain their place in a packed calendar. Therefore, just five months after the previous tournament finished, the third edition of the Shenzhen Masters took place in the second half of April.

Given the busy schedule of the leading players, it was not easy for the organizers to get players to Shenzhen this year. Nevertheless, with an average rating of 2754, not many people would doubt the status of this tournament as one of the super-category.

The field looked fairly familiar, as China's Ding Liren and Yu Yangyi and Dutch number one Anish Giri had played every edition so far. The format again was a double round-robin, with two Chinese stars and four foreign guests. As they competed under pristine playing conditions, one thing in particular stood out: compared to previous years, the Shenzhen Masters saw a lot more decisive results!

Another minor difference compared to previous editions was the playing venue. On the top floor of the five-star Shenzhen Castle Hotel in the Longgang District, the presidential suite had been transformed into a luxurious high-ceilinged playing room. Given the fact that the suite had multiple floors, the vibe was in a way comparable to that of the Candidates Tournament in Berlin, though there were surely many more spectators there.

Shenzhen is a remarkable city. Back in the 1970s, the town, bordering on Hong Kong, had a mere 30,000 inhabitants. In a remarkable move, the city was turned into a 'special economic zone' allowing foreign investors in 1980. This resulted in an incredible boom. By 2010, the number of inhabitants already exceeded 10 million, and the once modest border town is now a gigantic powerhouse. Buying an apartment in the city centre is not for the faint-hearted, as Shenzhen is one of the five most expensive cities in the world when it comes to real estate!

## Deceptively simple

Your reporter arrived a bit late, but upon landing in Shenzhen, I saw that Anish Giri had won his second-round game. That meant that with a start of 1½ out of 2, the bad form of Shamkir had been shaken off. I particularly like the phase between moves 19-25, where deceptively simple moves greatly increase White's advantage. Anish takes us through the how and why of his win against Harikrishna.

**NOTES BY**
**Anish Giri**

**Anish Giri**
**Pentala Harikrishna**
Shenzhen 2019 (2)
Italian Game, Giuoco Piano

After a somewhat unsettling result at the Gashimov Memorial in Shamkir – which ended less than a week before I arrived in China – I was happy to at least play a decent game in Round 1 of the Shenzhen Masters, drawing with Yu Yangyi after having had a comfortable position throughout the game.

For the second round, I felt ready to play a good game of chess and, fortunately for me, things went my way from start to finish.

**1.e4 e5 2.♘f3 ♘c6 3.♗c4 ♗c5 4.c3 ♘f6 5.d3 0-0 6.0-0 d5**

Harikrishna occasionally plays this ambitious system against the Italian. Not long before our game he failed to get anything as White against Vidit in the Prague Masters, so this didn't come as a shock to me.

**7.exd5 ♘xd5 8.♖e1** 8.a4 was all the rage at some point, but fashion

changes as people find new ideas to create and then to destroy.

**8...♗g4 9.♘bd2**

Hari started thinking a little here, and I began to suspect that he might not be familiar with all the latest news on this topic. To my pleasant surprise, since there had been a highly relevant game in this line in the Challengers group in Prague, played by Alexei Shirov, whose spectacular games are still followed closely by both the elite and the masses.

**9...♘b6 10.h3 ♗h5 11.♗b3**

This idea is not entirely new and I didn't come up with it myself. In fact, I had already profited from it in the 2018 World Rapid Championship, where I beat Inarkiev. There is the illusion that the d3-pawn is hanging, but in reality it is only starting here.

**11...♕xd3**

After some serious consideration Inarkiev thought better of taking the pawn in our rapid game.

**12.♘xe5**

**12...♗xd1?!**

Very tempting, especially when surprised. This had also been played by Markus Ragger, who I assume was

'Shenzhen is one of the five most expensive cities in the world when it comes to real estate!'

equally unfamiliar with the subtleties. The critical move is what Shirov played, 12...♕f5, when White goes 13.♘ef3 and then threatens to win a piece with g4, which Shirov was obviously happy to sacrifice.

**13.♘xd3 ♗xb3**

**14.axb3** I remembered there was a precedent to this move and that it gave White an advantage, but during the game I didn't see any reasons for not taking the b7-pawn.

It turns out that both the text-move and going for the pawn yield White a solid advantage: 14.♘xc5!? ♗c2 15.♘xb7 ♖fe8 16.♘f3 ♘a4. This puts up some resistance, but White can give back the b2- or c3-pawn and enjoy a better game. There are some drawish tendencies due to the opposite-coloured bishops, but with

knights on the board it's still a long way to go: 17.b3!? ♘xc3 18.♗d2 is yuck for Black.

**14...♗e7 15.b4**

Now that Sam Shankland has made this into a rule, we all understand why this move has to be played. A small step, and a giant improvement.

**15...a6** More natural than Ragger's 15...♖fe8. Here I had to make up stuff over the board, but it was pretty obvious that a knight has to go towards c5.

**16.♘e4** The reason I chose this move over the equally tempting 16.♘b3 was that the latter move gave Black the option of nestling his knight on c4, whereas now I will always have b2-b3. On e4, however, my knight is blocking the e-file and doesn't aim for the a5-square. Choices...

**16...♘d7** This felt too passive to me, but I can understand it: Black doesn't have weaknesses just yet and wants to just sit tight, hoping to eventually simplify matters. For now he prevents the ♘c5 jump. I had expected something along the lines of 16...♘d5 17.♘ec5 ♖fb8 (or 17...♖a7), while 16...♖fd8, with the idea of meeting 17.♘dc5 with 17...♖ab8, seems most sensible to me now.

**17.♗f4 ♖ac8** Defending the c7-pawn is no noble task for the rook.

**18.♖ad1** This move was played on general grounds, as I felt it was more natural than doubling on the e-file.

**18...♖fd8** I was happy to see this move, since it gives me g4 without Black being able to meet it with ...f5, slightly disturbing my e4-knight. The good thing about the g4-expansion is that it immediately opens up a mini-plan for me, as I can quickly follow it up with ♔g2, ♗g3, f4-f5.

I had not been looking forward to 18...h6 19.g4 (I could also wait a move with ♗h2 or ♔f1) 19...f5, though of course here, too, White is doing very well after 20.♘g3 fxg4 21.hxg4. I follow up with ♔g2 and the g3-knight will jump back in, either to e4 or sometimes even to f5.

18...f5 was also something to consider, when playing the knight to g5 looked like a natural reaction, but then Black can simplify a little and his king gets more breathing space: – 19.♘g5 ♗xg5 20.♗xg5 h6 21.♗f4 g5 22.♗h2. The c7-pawn is still a problem and 22...f4 doesn't work right now, even tactically, due to 23.♘xf4, when the d7-knight is

hanging. After 22...♖f7 23.f4!? Black also has problems.
– 19.♘d2!? is quite nasty, too, keeping more pieces on the board. Now ...g5/...f4 may shut down my bishop temporarily, but that feels like over-exposing, and if need be, the pawn-chain will easily be broken with g3.
**19.g4!**
There is really no other move here.

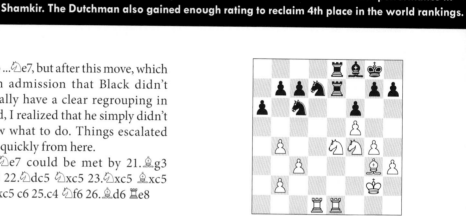

**19...♗f8** This is not too helpful. Actually, Black can't just sit and wait, because ♔g2, ♗g3 and f4-f5 are serious improvements. At this point, I would already consider something much more drastic, trying to trade some pieces or provoke some action. 19...f6 20.♔g2 ♔f7 is better than the game, but still doesn't change things. Probably the best defensive idea was 19...b6!? 20.♔g2 ♘f6, trying to trade some pieces or at least relocate them. Of course, with the rook still tied down to the c7-pawn, and the c6-knight not shining, the position remains very tough for Black. But that said, White still has a long way to go.
**20.♔g2**

**20...♖e8**
I was thinking that Black might want

to go ...♘e7, but after this move, which is an admission that Black didn't actually have a clear regrouping in mind, I realized that he simply didn't know what to do. Things escalated very quickly from here.
20...♘e7 could be met by 21.♗g3 ♘d5 22.♘dc5 ♘xc5 23.♘xc5 ♗xc5 24.bxc5 c6 25.c4 ♘f6 26.♗d6 ♖e8

**ANALYSIS DIAGRAM**

when Black would set up a fortress if there had been no rooks, but with one or both sets still on the board it is not going to be fun, especially after a rook or even the bishop lands on e7.
**21.♗g3 f6 22.f4 ♖e7** Something desperate needed to be done (perhaps ...a5 or something), but it was already pretty late at this point.
**23.f5 ♖ce8 24.♘f4!**

White now wins tactically, since the knight is going to land on e6 with devastating effect.
**24...♘d8** Allowing a cheap tactic, but at this point there was nothing even remotely close to a defence.
For instance, 24...♖xe4 25.♖xe4 ♖xe4 26.♖xd7 is lost, as ♘e6 is looming.
**25.♖xd7! ♖xd7 26.♘xf6+ gxf6 27.♖xe8 ♔f7 28.♖e3**

The last accurate move. Of course, everything is winning, but now the threat is ♖d3, when Black's position is really hopeless.

**28...♖d2+ 29.♔e2 ♖d1** Now White wins another pawn by force.

**30.♘e6 ♘xe6** 30...c6 would be bad news for the d8-knight.

**31.fxe6+ ♔e8 32.♗xc7**

If Black were just one pawn down, he would still have chances to defend, since the e6-pawn is rather weak, but with two extra pawns nothing can go wrong. The bishop ending wouldn't be too trivial, though, if we imagine that Black wins the e6-pawn; so I decided to avoid losing it.

**32...♖d3 33.♗f4 ♖d5 34.♔f3 ♔e7 35.♖e4 ♗g7 36.♗e3 f5 37.♗g5+ ♗f6 38.♗xf6+ ♔xf6**

**39.g5+** Pretending to blunder a final trick, which often happens just before the final move.

**39...♔xg5 40.♖e3!** Now the black rook has to go to e8, when White will eventually get the king to f4 and force a won pawn ending. After 40.e7, 40...fxe4+ 41.♔xe4 ♖d1! would have been awkward. Black resigned.

■ ■ ■

## Four wins on the trot

If you think that this was perhaps the start of a horrible tournament for Harikrishna, I can tell you that it was quite the opposite! In Round 3, 'Hari' won a better endgame against Richard Rapport, Round 5 saw him do the same against Yu Yangyi, and in Round 6, his victim was Dmitry Jakovenko, again in the endgame. Hari actually won four games in a row, as Round 4 saw him defeating top-seed Ding Liren... from a slightly better endgame!

NOTES BY
**Pentala Harikrishna**

**Pentala Harikrishna
Ding Liren**
Shenzhen 2019 (4)
Ruy Lopez, Anti-Marshall

This was the second time I played in the Shenzhen Masters. I also took part in 2017, in the first edition. In 2018, I played in the Chinese League several times, and at least two times the venue was in Shenzhen or nearby places. Even though jet lag is an issue, the good memories from that season in the Chinese League compensated ☺.

The conditions in the Shenzhen Masters were excellent, and the activities on the rest day were cool and helped me to relax. I arrived only one day early, something which I would not recommend to anyone!!

For my game against Ding Liren I was in fighting mode. The biggest question was which opening I would see. Ding Liren is famous for an undefeated streak last year of 100 games! In the end, I decided to go for an opening that gained popularity in the 2018 Candidates, but as expected he was ready for it.

**1.e4 e5**
Sometimes he plays the Caro-Kann or the Sicilian. The Marshall is his main choice.

**2.♘f3 ♘c6 3.♗b5 a6 4.♗a4 ♘f6 5.0-0 ♗e7 6.♖e1 b5 7.♗b3 0-0**

**8.d3** The previous time I tried another anti-Marshall against him, 8.a4, and although I got a good position in the 2017 Shenzhen Masters, I blundered and eventually lost.

**8...d6 9.♗d2!?** This move was introduced at the top level by Grischuk in the Candidates against Aronian. The main idea is stopping Black's ...♘a5. followed by ...c5.

**9...♗g4** The main move in this position. I had expected that Ding would go for something active.

9...♗b7 was played by Karjakin against Surya Ganguly in the Kolkata Tata Steel rapid and blitz event. Definitely an interesting alternative for Black.

**10.c3**
10.h3 is dubious because of the following variation. Black equalizes by exchanging pieces: 10...♗xf3 11.♕xf3 ♘d4 12.♕d1 a5 13.c3 ♘xb3.
**10...♘a5 11.♗c2 c5 12.h3 ♗h5 13.♗c1 ♘c6**
The first new move for me and quite logical indeed. Until 13...♘c6 we had blitzed out our moves, because both

of us had been ready for this variation – but he was probably a bit more ready than me ☺.

**14.♘bd2 d5**

**15.♘f1**

It would be too greedy to go for the pawn: 15.exd5?! ♘xd5 16.g4 ♗g6 17.♘xe5 ♘xe5 18.♖xe5 ♗f6 19.♖e1 b4, and Marshall players wouldn't have to think twice if they could get such a position as Black. Black is already better, even though White is up a pawn.

During the game I found it hard to decide between the move I played and 15.g4, when, as detailed analysis showed, White has good attacking chances. Best would be 15...♗g6 16.♘h4 d4 17.♘df3 c4!? (Black can also play slowly, 17...♘d7, when after 18.♘f5 the position is unclear) 18.dxc4 bxc4 19.♘xg6 hxg6 20.♗a4 ♖c8 21.♗xc6 ♖xc6 22.cxd4! exd4 23.e5 ♘d5 24.♕xd4 ♘b4 25.♖e2, with a white edge.

**15...dxe4 16.dxe4 ♕xd1 17.♗xd1**

**17...♖fd8** I don't think this is inaccurate, but I like 17...c4 more, since it is more to the point. The engine

In the end he had to settle for second best, but with five wins (and four in a row!) Pentala Harikrishna will not easily forget the 2019 Shenzhen Masters.

found a nice idea, which initially did not make any sense to me. In order to execute this idea, the d8-square should be vacant, as Black wants to bring his c6-knight to e6 via d8: 17...c4! 18.♘g3 ♗xf3 19.♗xf3 g6 and the knight will go to e6. And if White brings his c1-bishop to e3, Black will exchange it. For the rest Black is controlling all important squares.

**18.♘g3 ♗g6** After 18...♗xf3 19.♗xf3 g6 20.♘f1 c4 21.♘e3 Black will find it hard to reroute his knight to e6.

**19.♘h4! ♘d7**

19...♘xe4 20.♘xg6 loses to 20...♘xg3 21.♘xe7+, of course.

I evaluated the position after 19...♘xe4 20.♘xe4 ♘xe4 21.♘f5 ♗f6 22.a4 to be slightly more pleasant for White.

**20.♘gf5!**

After 20.♘xg6?! hxg6 White cannot have the ♘f5 tempo as in the game, and this might be crucial.

**20...♗f8 21.b3!** I did not want to allow Black to get ...c4 and ...♘c5. Another important thing is that after ...c4 it would be hard for White to break on the queenside.

**21...b4!?**

Probably simpler was 21...c4, with a similar motif as in the game. After 22.bxc4 ♘c5 23.♘xg6 hxg6 24.♘e3 b4 25.♘d5 bxc3 26.♘xc3 ♖ab8 Black has excellent compensation.

**22.♗b2** After 22.cxb4 ♘xb4 23.♘xg6 hxg6 24.♘e3 ♘d3 25.♘f1 ♘xc1 26.♖xc1 ♘b6 my assessment is 'equal', whereas the engine thinks White is better. The reader can decide whom to trust ☺.

**22...c4** I had anticipated this sacrifice, feeling that Black should be doing fine for the sacrificed pawn.
**23.bxc4 ♘c5 24.♗c2 ♖d2 25.♖ac1 ♗xf5 26.♘xf5 ♖ad8 27.♔f1**

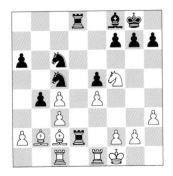

**27...a5?!**

The simplest way to equalize was 27...♘d3. I don't think Ding missed it. He was probably already playing for an advantage, and if nothing worked out, he can make a draw at any time. Sometimes this works well, but in this case he lost his sense of danger. After 28.♗xd3 ♖8xd3 29.♖e2 ♖d1+ 30.♖xd1 ♖xd1+ 31.♖e1 ♖d2 chances would be equal.

**28.♘e3 ♘d3 29.♗xd3 ♖xb2**

After 29...♖8xd3 30.♖e2, the d1-square is controlled and White is simply a pawn up.

**30.♖e2 ♖xe2**

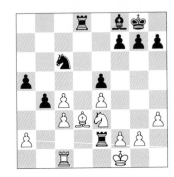

Accompanied by a draw offer, which was allowed as from move 30. I saw no risk for White and came to the same conclusion: if something went wrong, I could make draw at any time ☺. So I decided to continue for a few more moves!

**31.♗xe2 ♖d2**

Stronger was 31...bxc3!, and White has no way to improve his position. The best White can get is an opposite-coloured bishops ending a pawn up: 32.♖xc3 ♗c5 33.♘d5 ♘d4 34.♖c1 ♖b8 35.♗d3 ♔f8 36.♖b1 ♖xb1+ 37.♗xb1.

**32.cxb4**

**32...♗xb4**

32...axb4! 33.♖c2 ♖xc2 34.♘xc2 ♘a5 should be a draw as well. Since White cannot allow ...b3 and the only way to defend is ♘a1, he does not really have a winning plan here.

**33.c5!** Most likely overlooked by my opponent. He probably thought that White would have to repeat moves after 33...♗a3.

**33...♗a3**

**34.♖d1?!**

I should have played 34.♖b1!. I saw this move and felt it was not enough to win. When I look at the position now, it is clear that White is completely winning. I have no explanation for why I did not go for this move: 34...♗xc5 35.♖c1 ♗xe3 36.fxe3 (36.♖xc6 ♗g5!, with equality) 36...♘e7 37.a4 ♖a2 38.♖c7 ♔f8 39.♗b5.

**34...♖xd1+ 35.♔xd1 ♗xc5 36.♘c4**

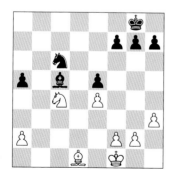

I thought that this position was quite unpleasant for Black and that White would win a pawn. Surprisingly, I expected 36...♗d4 to be the main move for Black and my opponent duly played it. When I turned on the engine, it told me that almost any move is fine here, except 36...♗d4. If

During the free hours the hosts organized a multitude of activities for the players, including golf. Ding Liren takes his time to decide how to hit the ball and where to.

anyone has an explanation for this, I am waiting to hear it ☺.

**36...♗d4?!**

After 36...♔f8 37.♗a4 ♘b4 38.♘xe5 ♗d4 39.♘c4 ♘xa2 40.♘xa5 ♘b4, White will play, but Black's drawing chances are quite high.

**37.♗a4 ♘b4 38.a3 ♘d3 39.♘xa5**

I have no idea whether this position is won or drawn. Defending it is quite unpleasant for Black. White needs to play some accurate moves to slowly improve his pawn and at the same time bring his king forward. I think it was best for Black to just stay put, instead of moving the knight from c5. In the rest of the game my technique is far from perfect.

**39...♘c5 40.♗c6 ♔f8 41.♘c4**

♔e7 42.f3 ♘d8 43.♔e2 ♔c7 44.♔d5 f6 45.♗g8 h6 46.h4 ♘b7 47.a4 ♘d6 48.♘d2 ♔b6 49.♘b3 ♗c3 50.♗d5 ♗b4 51.h5 ♗c3 52.♔d3 ♗e1 53.♔c2 ♗f2 54.♘c1 f5 55.♘d3 ♗g3 56.♔b3 fxe4 57.♗xe4 ♘e8 58.♔b4 ♘f6 59.a5+ ♔a7 60.♗g6 ♘d5+ 61.♔b5 ♘c7+ 62.♔a4 ♘d5 63.♗e4 ♘f6 64.♘b4 ♘xh5 65.♘c6+ ♔a8 66.♘xe5+ ♔b8 67.♘c6+ ♔c7 68.♔b5

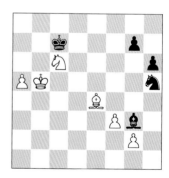

**68...♘f6?** Both of us had missed 68...♘f4!, and I am not sure whether White is winning here. Many of the moves were made in time-pressure. After 69.a6 ♗f2 70.g3 ♘h5 71.g4 ♘f4 it looks like a draw.

**69.♘d4! ♘e8 70.a6 ♘d6+ 71.♔c5 ♗f2**

**72.♔d5**

After so many adventures I did not want to give up my a-pawn, so I chose a slightly longer path. But 72.a7 was winning, too: 72...♗xd4+ 73.♔xd4 ♘b5+ 74.♔e5 ♘xa7 75.♔f5 ♘d6 76.♔g6 ♔e5 77.♔xg7 h5 78.♔g6 ♔f4 79.♔xh5 ♔g3 80.♔g5, and wins.

**72...♘c8 73.♘f5 ♘b6+ 74.♔e6 ♘d7 75.♔f7 g5 76.♘xh6 ♔b6 77.♗b7 ♗e3 78.♔e6 ♘c5+ 79.♔f5**

And with the g-pawn about to fall, my opponent resigned.

This game was far from perfect, but any win gives a good feeling and I had won my Round 5 and 6 games as well. Then came the unbeatable and rock-solid Anish Giri to spoil my streak ☺.

■ ■ ■

For one reason or another, Shenzhen has not yet proven to be very fertile ground for Yu Yangyi. China's number two player finished in last place with three losses and seven draws. What happened in his game against Anish Giri was incomprehensible.

**Anish Giri**
**Yu Yangyi**
Shenzhen 2019 (6)

position after 70.♔f3

Black can simply stick his knight on e6 and await developments forever. The position is a fortress.
Instead, there followed **70...♘d3?! 71.♗d4 ♘e1+!? 72.♔e2 ♘c2 73.♗c5**

and the black knight got trapped.
A few more adventures ensued, with Anish gracefully allowing the knight to jump back to e6, but by this point dark spirits had taken a firm hold of this game and on move 102, Yu Yangyi resigned.

Rapport fared better, as he produced a decent 50% score. If having Richard in a tournament was a guarantee for crazy games in the past, as of late he has embraced the Hungarian school of sound technical play. In the final round, he missed a huge chance to lift himself to +1, but as Richie told me during the closing dinner, he is mostly just delighted to get a chance to play in tournaments like Wijk aan Zee, earlier this year, and now Shenzhen.

As Harikrishna already pointed out himself, his amazing winning streak was finally stopped by Anish.

**Pentala Harikrishna**
**Anish Giri**
Shenzhen 2019 (7)

position after 34...♕d4

Anish had been under immense pressure the entire game, after a rare lapse in the opening, a ♗b5-Sicilian. The diagrammed position shows what was perhaps Harikrishna's biggest chance.

**35.♕b3?** Instead of the text-move, 35.♕b5! keeps an eye on both the c6- and the e5-pawn. Now 35...♕a1+ 36.♔h2 leads nowhere, and 35...♘d6 36.♕a5! (36.♕b8 ♘c8 37.♕xc8 ♕xb4 38.♕d7 should also do) 36...♕d1+ 37.♔h2 ♕d4 38.♗c5 ♕f4+ 39.g3 ♕f6 40.♕a8 ♕e6 41.♕d8 leads to Black's collapse.

**35...♕a1+ 36.♔h2 ♕c1!**
Highlighting White's error on move 35. From here on in, the queen threatens perpetual check while keeping an eye on the c-pawn.

**37.♕f3**

**37...♕f4+**

37...♕c4! would perhaps have been a bit simpler, but Anish had correctly assessed the upcoming endgame to be drawn. Pentala pushed hard for another 30 moves, but in vain.

**38.♕xf4 exf4 39.♗d2 g5 40.♗a5 ♔g6 41.c7 ♘d6 42.♗b4 ♘c8 43.♗g1 ♔f5 44.♔f1 ♔e6 45.♔e2 ♔d7 46.♗f8 h5 47.♔f3 ♔xc7 48.♔e4 ♘b6 49.♔f5 g4 50.♔xf4 gxh3 51.gxh3**

And a draw on move 66.

**Another fascinating endgame**

Anish's holding this endgame would prove pivotal for the final standings. Going into the last round, Harikrishna had a half-point lead over Giri, who was his only pursuer. Harikrishna was to play Ding Liren with the black pieces. Ding had suffered from a somewhat sluggish start and certainly could not be satisfied with the 50% score that he entered the last round with. And again this game also came down to a fascinating endgame!

**Ding Liren**
**Pentala Harikrishna**
Shenzhen 2019 (10)

position after 35.♘b3

White is better because of his control of the c-file, but for now it is all within limits.

**35...b6** Better was 35...g5!, with the idea to meet 36.♘d2 with 36...♖xd2+ 37.♖xd2 f4!, when Black's counterplay on the kingside guarantees a draw.

**36.♘d2 ♘g5?!** Now it becomes very unpleasant. Here, too, 36...♖xd2+ 37.♖xd2 g5! was called for. Here's a sample line: 38.♖dc2 f4 39.♖c7 ♖f6 40.♔e2 f3+ 41.♔e1 ♖fe6, and this is just a fortress.

**37.h4 ♘e6**

**38.♘b1!** The knight moves on to greener pastures. First to c3, from where it attacks d5. Note that it's very hard for Black to get active counterplay. It's possible that White is already winning at this point.

**38...h6 39.♘c3 g5 40.hxg5 hxg5 41.♘a2 f4 42.♘b4 ♔f6 43.♖c8 ♔f5 44.♖h8 ♖f7**

**45.♔e2**

45.♘c6!? was the fast way to cash in, in order to always have a check on e5. Black will be unable to create play on the kingside.

**What to do at an ice hockey rink? Make your opponents believe that you're working on the Nimzowitsch Defence, as Ding Liren and Yu Yangyi seem to suggest?**

**45...f3+ 46.♔d2 ♘f8 47.♖c8**
47.♖c6!? ♖d8 48.♖ch6 may look like an odd manoeuvre, but once you see the knight landing on c6 on the next move, it's easy to understand that White is utterly dominant.
**47...♘g6** 47...♘h7 48.♘c6 ♘f6 threatens ...♘g4, but 49.♘e5 stops that just in time.
**48.♖h6 ♘e7 49.♖xd6 ♘xc8**

**50.♖xd5+**
50.♖d8! now, or on the next move, would have saved Ding some headaches. The lines are very straightforward: 50...♘e7 51.♖d7 ♔e6 52.♖xa7 ♖h7 53.♘c6, and wins, or 50...♖h7 51.♖xc8 ♖h2 52.♖c2 ♖xf2+ 53.♔e1!, and Black is forced to exchange rooks.
**50...♔g4 51.♘c6 ♔h3!**
Having missed clear wins, White now suddenly has to deal with a fearless king. Donner already wrote about the strength of the king in the endgame, and this is a perfect example!
**52.♘e5**

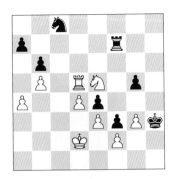

**52...♖f6!?**
Also 52...♖c7!? 53.♖d7 ♖xd7 54.♘xd7 ♔g2 55.♔e1 ♘d6 is probably enough for a draw. After 56.♘f6 ♔g1 57.♘h7

♘f7 58.d5 ♔g2 59.d6 ♘xd6 60.♘g5 ♘c4! 61.♘xe4 ♘e5 62.♔d2 ♘g4 63.♔e1 ♘e5,

ANALYSIS DIAGRAM

despite the two extra pawns, it is impossible for White to make any progress.
**53.♖d8 ♘d6 54.♔c3 ♘f5 55.♖h8+ ♔g2 56.♘g4 ♖f7 57.♖h2+ ♔g1 58.♔c4**
This is what Ding must have been counting on. The knight on g4 does a fantastic job keeping the kingside together, while the king will try to match its counterpart by entering Black's position.

**58...♖d7!**
Thou shalt not pass!
**59.♖h5 ♖d6**
Here 59...♘xe3+! 60.fxe3 f2 61.♘h2 ♖c7+ 62.♔d5 ♖c1 63.♔xe4 ♔g2 64.d5 ♖h1 narrowly makes a draw: 65.♖xg5 ♔xh2 66.♖f5 f1♕ 67.♖xf1 ♖xf1 68.d6 ♖d1 69.♔e5 ♔xg3 70.♔e6 ♖e1!.
But to illustrate just how fine Black's position is at this point, even 59...♔f1!? 60.♖xg5 ♘d6+!, and now both 61.♔d5 ♘f7+ 62.♔e6 ♘xg5+ 63.♔xd7 ♘h3! and 61.♔b4

♖c7 62.♖g6 ♘b7! offer sufficient counterplay.

**60.d5**

**60...♖g6** The computer still insists that 60...♖d7 61.♖xg5 ♖c7+ 62.♔b4 ♘d6 is 0.00, but it feels like this is harder to play with Black.

**61.♖h7 ♖d6**

**62.a5!**

Now Ding breaks through. The execution is swift.

**62...bxa5 63.♖xa7 ♘h6 64.♔c5 ♖d8 65.♘xh6 ♔xf2 66.♘f5 ♔g2 67.♖xa5 f2 68.♖a2 ♔f3 69.♖xf2+ ♔xf2**

The passed pawns decide.

**70.b6 ♖b8 71.d6 ♔f3 72.d7 ♖f8**

Black resigned.

---

This was a heavy loss for Hari, but I admired the way he carried himself after the game. Four wins in a row is a feat that I predict will not be repeated any time soon in Shenzhen, and after a tough couple of months it was good to see India's number two back in form!

The outcome of the above game meant that a draw or a win would yield Anish Giri the so hotly desired tournament victory. His opponent, Dmitry Jakovenko, had had a frustrating tournament so far with two losses and seven draws.

**NOTES BY Anish Giri**

**Anish Giri**
**Dmitry Jakovenko**
Shenzhen 2019 (10)
Catalan Opening, Closed Variation

**1.c4**

I am curious to know if anyone will ever figure out why this game started with 1.c4. In any case, later on we transpose to a line of the Catalan.

**1...♘f6 2.g3 e6 3.♗g2 d5 4.♘f3 ♗e7 5.d4 0-0 6.♘c3 dxc4 7.♘e5 c5**

My opponent had played this endgame against Richard Rapport in one of the earlier rounds. I had some small questions here, and I thought this was a good opportunity to ask them.

**8.dxc5 ♕xd1+ 9.♘xd1 ♗xc5**

**10.0-0**

Sophisticated moves like 10.♘e3, 10.♘c3 and 10.♗d2 are more trendy, and in fact I even played one of them against Topalov in the 2016 Candidates Tournament.

This time, though, I had a different idea, which only works in the 10.0-0 move order.

**10...♘c6**

My opponent started spending a lot of time after this. This was good news, because if Black is well prepared in a position like this, and has refreshed all move order trickery before the game, the chances are high that White's symbolic endgame advantage will peter out – even more so when facing a good technician like Dmitry Jakovenko. To be honest, if not for the result of this game, one could say that my opening choice was pretty poor.

**11.♗xc6!?**

This 'cool' capture had been played only once before, by Vladimir Malakhov against Peter Leko. As a rule, White treasures his Catalan bishop, but this is an endgame, the knight on e5 is pretty good, too, and chess is a concrete game.

11.♘xc6 bxc6 12.♗e3 is more natural, but after 12...♗xe3 13.♘xe3 Black gets quick counterplay with ...♗a6 and ...♖ab8 – in random order. White is one tempo short here of securing a serious positional advantage, which is pretty much the story of a Catalan player's life.

**11...bxc6 12.♗e3 ♗b6**

A good resource. White can now eliminate Black's bishop pair, but that would dramatically improve Black's pawn structure. So far, we are

# 'White is one tempo short of securing a serious positional advantage, which is pretty much the story of a Catalan player's life.'

still following Malakhov-Leko, so I wouldn't have been surprised if we had reached this position relatively quicker.

**13.♗xb6!?**
A counter-intuitive, rather innocent new move, which I was pretty sure would come as a surprise, given that neither the engines consider it dangerous nor does it look dangerous to the human eye. However, when browsing one of the files I had made for Vladimir Kramnik (as his second for the 2018 Candidates tournament – ed.), I realized that I once again had sold him a very ugly position as equality and had to check things all over again.
13.♘xc4 ♗a6 14.♖c1 ♘d5 15.♖e1 ♖fd8 16.b3 ♖ac8 17.♗d2 c5 18.♘db2 ♘b4 19.♗xb4 cxb4 20.♘xb6 axb6 21.♖xc8 ♖xc8 22.♘d3 ♗xd3 23.exd3 ♖c2 was a very well-played draw in Malakhov-Leko, Germany 2016. Black had an ugly pawn on c5, nicely blocked by the knight, but eventually profited from the bishop pair, forcing White to trade his knights.

**13...axb6**

**14.♘c3**

This is a very clever move, as White is postponing the decision what pawn to take, depending on what pawn Black will choose to protect. In fact, if you take ♘xc4, Black wants to go ...♗a6, while if you take ♘xc6 he wants to go ...♗b7, so in a way White kind of gains a tempo by waiting for the bishop move.

**14...♗d7**
Protecting the c6-pawn feels much more solid, but there are also other ways to try to defend this position.

**15.♖fd1 ♖fd8**
The engine indicates a slight preference to defending the bishop from the side, which over the board seemed far less obvious to me: 15...♖a7!?, with the idea that after 16.♘xc4 there is 16...♖b8 in one go, and now the computer does have a point, since the extra move ...♖a7 can only be helpful.

**16.♘xc4**

**16...b5?!**
To be honest, I didn't recall what I had prepared here. Maybe I didn't look at this natural (but not very good, 16...♖db8!? seemed better) move at all.
At first, I was briefly puzzled, since the tempting moves 17.♘b6 and 17.♘d6 seemed to lead to some very drawish endgames by force. Fortunately, though, the position wasn't too complicated and I managed to

find a simple way to maintain the pressure.

**17.♘e5!**
After 17.♘b6 ♖a6 18.♘xd7 ♖xd7 19.♖xd7 ♘xd7 20.♖d1 ♖a7 Black is totally fine.
17.♘d6 looked like the best move for a while, preparing ♘e4-c5, but here Black gets more time than in the game, because White's position is slightly less stable: 17...♗e8. Now the a2-pawn is hanging after 18.♘ce4, so White has to spend an extra tempo: 18.a3 ♘d5 19.♘de4 ♔f8, followed by ...♔e7, etc. (pushing the f- and e-pawns forward), when it's not much for White.

**17...♗e8**
17...b4 is met by 18.♘e4! ♘xe4 19.♘xd7, which is important. Black's b4-pawn is going to fall, because White controls the c5-square.

**18.♖xd8! ♖xd8 19.♘d3**

When in China… Anish Giri tests his table tennis skills against Ding Liren (watch that penhold grip!). The chessboards seem to pose an additional challenge.

**22...⬜c8 23.♘e4**
Here I found a little cheapo, but my opponent noticed it just in time.
**23...c5** Black's defensive attempt kind of makes sense. Now the plan is to meet ♘d6 with ...⬜c6, when it would seem that the best White can do is drop back to c4; but then Black would have visibly made some small progress. But, oh, no, the cheapos.
**24.♘d6**

**24...⬜b8** After a while my opponent visibly started getting upset, which I assumed was caused by the fact that he had noticed the cheapo at the very last moment. The problem is also that, even if he doesn't fall for it, the whole defensive setup stops working and the c5-pawn eventually falls. Indeed, 24...⬜c6 25.♘xf7! was a very nice one!
**25.⬜c7 ♚e7 26.♘b7!**
The knight is doing well here.
**26...♚f6**
Instead, 26...♚f8 felt stronger, when the king would be less exposed, the e8-bishop better protected and ...f6 still possible. But Black was doing very badly already.

**27.b3!**

This looked very good, but now that I think about it, the immediate 19.a4 also deserved attention.

**19...♚f8?!**
This felt wrong, mostly because after 20.a4 and 21.⬜xa4 my position suddenly looked extremely good to me.
I briefly considered moves like 19...e5, 19...c5, 19...♘d5, but as none of them worked, it seemed the best move was 19...⬜a8, preventing White from activating his rook. Here I had a wide range of options, but I think I was leaning towards 20.b3!?, preparing a4 and keeping more pieces on the board.
**20.a4** Here I got really enthusiastic about my chances.
**20...bxa4 21.⬜xa4**

The pawn structure is almost symmetrical, and the c6-pawn is not much of a weakness just yet. But there is no hope for Black to further simplify the game, because the b2-pawn will forever be covered by the perfect knight on d3. White also has easy ways to improve his position, whereas if Black tries to activate his e8-bishop, which can only be done by moving the f-pawn, the e6-pawn will probably come under attack and the tactics may work against him. Basically, Black is kind of busted.
**21...♘d7 22.⬜a7!** A good move, trying to sneak in behind the c6-pawn. What was also very important was to avoid playing the tempting b4-push, which would temporarily fix the c6-pawn, but give Black a real target after the knight came back to d5.

## 'It was only the fact that the simul was stopped due to time restraints that prevented the boys from mating me.'

I was tempted to try and win this tactically, but, surprisingly, after 27.f4 c4 28.♘f2 e5! I didn't see a forced win, for the simple reason that there wasn't one.

**27...g5** After 27...♖a8 28.f3 ♖a7 the pin fails completely: 29.♘d6!.

**28.f3!**
White can improve his position for now, because taking on c5 can wait.

**28...h6 29.♔f2 ♖a8 30.♘d6**
I could have taken on c5, of course, but I decided on a more technical approach, as having rooks on the board could potentially lead to a rook ending in which accidents could happen. I'm not sure what was cleaner, but in any case, the choice I made didn't spoil anything. By the way, White's position is a technical win by now, which did not feel this way but is also confirmed by the engine.

But let's look at what would happen if I took the pawn: 30.♘bxc5 ♘xc5 31.♘xc5 ♔g6 32.♘e4 (32.♖b7!, and pushing the b-pawn should be good. If need be there is ♖b6 to take away the c6-square from the bishop) 32...♖a6, stopping ♘d6, when I thought Black would still be fighting.

**30...♔e7 31.♖c8**

I must be honest – I liked the perversion of this. This briefly looks as if White ruins everything, but then suddenly it turns out that the c5-pawn will fall.

**31...♖xc8 32.♘xc8+ ♔d8 33.♘d6 ♔e7 34.♘b7**

**34...♘b6** I thought 34...c4 would maybe offer more saving chances, while trading the knights should lose quickly. Actually, what my opponent did worked out well, since he got

chances to save the game when he shouldn't have.

**35.♘bxc5 f6 36.f4 gxf4 37.gxf4**
Here I still felt the win should come naturally, since the b6-knight is about to be dominated.

**37...f5** A shocker, but in fact a good desperate attempt. Now all I need to do is get my king to d4, but for that I had to see a cute tactical nuance.

**38.♔e3 ♗h5**

**39.♘b4?** Not seeing how to get the king to d4, I got obsessed over not allowing ...♘d5+, pushing my king back to d2, although I realized much, much later in the game that this wasn't a problem at all.

Actually, what I shouldn't have allowed is the black knight coming to e4: 39.♘a4! ♘d5+, and now:

**ANALYSIS DIAGRAM**

A) 40.♔d4! ♗xe2 41.♘c3!. This is very beautiful. The pawn endings are all lost for Black, and he is also

| Shenzhen 2019 | | | | | 1 | 2 | 3 | 4 | 5 | 6 | cat. XXI TPR |
|---|---|---|---|---|---|---|---|---|---|---|---|
| 1 Anish Giri | IGM | NED | 2797 | | ** | 1 ½ | ½ ½ | ½ ½ | ½ 1 | ½ 1 | 6½ | 2855 |
| 2 Pentala Harikrishna | IGM | IND | 2723 | | 0 ½ | ** | 1 0 | 1 0 | ½ 1 | 1 1 | 6 | 2832 |
| 3 Ding Liren | IGM | CHN | 2809 | | ½ ½ | 0 1 | ** | ½ ½ | 1 ½ | ½ ½ | 5½ | 2779 |
| 4 Richard Rapport | IGM | HUN | 2726 | | ½ ½ | 0 1 | ½ ½ | ** | ½ ½ | ½ ½ | 5 | 2759 |
| 5 Dmitry Jakovenko | IGM | RUS | 2719 | | ½ 0 | ½ 0 | 0 ½ | ½ ½ | ** | ½ ½ | 3½ | 2651 |
| 6 Yu Yangyi | IGM | CHN | 2751 | | ½ 0 | 0 0 | ½ ½ | ½ ½ | ½ ½ | ** | 3½ | 2644 |

doomed to lose the bishop vs knight ending, despite the pawns equality. The win is straightforward: White distracts Black's king with his b-pawn and wins the three kingside pawns. Total control: 41...♘xc3 42.♔xc3 ♔d6 43.♔d4.

B) 40.♔d2 obviously wins as well. I get the position that I eventually got in the game, only after far too much shuffling: 40...♔d6 41.♘c3 (41.e3 ♘f6 42.♘c3 is what I should have played if I had not seen the pawn-sac idea. I got this setup towards the end of the game, but at this point I was still hoping to get my king to d4, ahead of the knights).

**39...♔d6 40.♘b7+ ♔c7 41.♘c5 ♔d6**

For a while I tried to find some zugzwang situation to get my king to d4, but after realizing that it would never work I abandoned this ambitious plan and dropped my king back to d2. Then eventually (when I realized that a draw would also give me first place) I pushed stuff forward, regrouped a few times and won the game. It got a little greasy, though, because we got into time-trouble and my manoeuvres felt clumsy. So, surely, with a better defence, the result would still have been very much in doubt, but I will spare you the details.

**42.♘cd3 ♘d7 43.h3 ♘f6 44.♘e5 ♘e4 45.♘a2 ♔d5 46.♘c4 ♔c5 47.♘b2 ♔d6 48.♘c4+ ♔c5 49.♘b2 ♔d6 50.♘d3 ♔d5 51.♘e5 ♔c5 52.♘c1 ♘c3 53.♘ed3+ ♔d5 54.♘f2 ♔c5 55.♔d2 ♘d5 56.e3 ♘f6**

**57.♘cd3+ ♔d5 58.♘e5 ♔c5 59.♘fd3+ ♔d5 60.♘b4+ ♔c5 61.♘a2 ♘e4+ 62.♔c2 ♘d6 63.♘c3 ♗e8 64.♘d3+ ♔b6 65.♔d2 ♗c6 66.h4 ♗g2 67.♔e2 ♗b7 68.♘a4+ ♔b5 69.♘c3+**

**69...♔b6 70.♔d2 ♗g2 71.♘a4+ ♔c6 72.♘e5+ ♔b5 73.♔c2 ♗e8 74.♘c3+ ♔c5 75.♘d3+ ♔d6 76.b4 ♘f6 77.♘e5 ♗f1 78.♔d2 h5 79.♘d3 ♗g2 80.b5 ♘g4 81.♘a4 ♘f6 82.♔c3 ♘e4+ 83.♔d4**

**83...♘d2 84.♘e5 ♘b3+ 85.♔c3 ♘c1 86.♔b4 ♔c7 87.b6+ ♔b7 88.♔b5 ♗f1+ 89.♔c5 ♘e2 90.♔d6 ♗g3 91.♘d7 ♗g2 92.♘ac5+ ♔c8 93.♘xe6 ♘f1 94.e4 ♗xe4 95.♘xe4 fxe4 96.♘c5 ♘d2 97.♔d5**
Black resigned.

■ ■ ■

And so Anish took clear first! Messages from all over the world poured in with congratulations. The World Champion also chimed in: 'I would like to offer my quite insincere congratulations to Anish for his win.' When I saw Anish compli-

So that's what the future looks like. Erwin l'Ami discovered that the King's Indian and the Sicilian may stay en vogue for a while.

menting Carlsen on his recent streak of victories on Twitter a few days later, it was clear to me there is a bromance in the making!

### The future

On the day before their departure, the players were asked to give a simul to talented kids. Since Pentala Harikrishna had to catch a flight, I volunteered to help out. Little did I know the trouble I would get myself into! Two boys (see picture), both barely able to reach the other side of the board, went all out on me. It was only the fact that the simul was stopped due to time restraints that prevented the boys from mating me. One in a sharp King's Indian, the other one in an equally tough Najdorf Sicilian. Clearly, a new generation of Chinese top players is on their way! ■

# 9TH GIBRALTAR

# JUNIOR INTERNATIONAL CHESS FESTIVAL

**COACHING TEAM INCLUDES:**
GM David Howell

**READY TO PLAY CHESS?**

## £15,000 PRIZE MONEY

**Arrival 15th August & Departure 20th August 2019**
4 Star Venue: The Caleta Hotel, Gibraltar
Categories: under 16 years & under 12 years

FIDE Rated, 6 Rounds Per Event ♟ Maximum FIDE Elo of 2300, May 1st 2019 ♟ Meet & Greet
GM Coaching & Masterclasses ♟ Blitz & Simultaneous ♟ Excursions ♟ Gala Dinner & Prize Giving

**NEW!** - PARALLEL INVITE-ONLY EVENT(S) FOR 17-18 YEAR OLDS, PLEASE ENQUIRE!

Website: www.gibchess.com/junior   Further information: chess@caletahotel.gi
Bookings: cathy.popham@caletahotel.gi  ▶ 📷 f 𝕏

PARTNERED BY
GSLA.gi   GIBRALT
VISITGIBRALT

# MAXIMize your Tactics

## with Maxim Notkin

## Find the best move in the positions below

Solutions on page 63

1. White to play

2. White to play

3. Black to play

4. Black to play

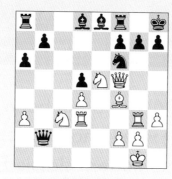

5. White to play

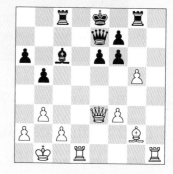

6. White to play

7. Black to play

8. Black to play

9. Black to play

## A peek into the sorcerer's universe
# Bronstein's Magic

RON KROON

**Two chess legends that liked to talk and challenge conventional wisdom: David Bronstein and Hein Donner at the start of the 1968 IBM tournament in Amsterdam.**

David Bronstein (1924-2006) has often been praised for his creativity and brilliance. But what was it that made his genius so special? Inspired by his wife and the modern classic *The Sorcerer's Apprentice* (or vice versa), **MIHAIL MARIN** went looking for answers.

A highly original player and a chess philosopher, David Bronstein is widely known as an outstanding grandmaster who, in 1951, played for the world title against Botvinnik (who drew the match and retained his title). Bronstein's successes are countless, yet his games and a lot of what made them special remained clouded in mystery for me for quite a long time. Sure, I had enjoyed analysing some of his games (mostly from the 1953 Zurich Candidates tournament; see for instance my article in New In Chess 2011/5), but without fully understanding what really made him so strong.

It was only by chance that I recently got a deeper insight into his creative universe.

During my long working days on articles and books, my wife Mariya usually sits opposite to me at the same

## 'Each game or fragment, together with Bronstein's stories and comments, creates the sensation of a fairy tale.'

desk, playing over games from books. She does this in the most constructive way, closing the book after each move and trying to figure out the continuation herself.

One morning, noticing that I took a short break from my typing, she asked me: 'What would you play here with Black?' I first looked at the book she was holding in her hands: David Bronstein's and Tom Fürstenberg's *Uchenik Charodeja*, the Russian translation of *The Sorcerer's Apprentice*, a book she had given to me as a present, but which I had not found the time to look through.

In the meantime, things have changed, because later we spent many hours studying the book, usually on terraces during tournaments, as a mutually agreed best way to prepare for the next game. It's a special book. Each game or fragment, together with Bronstein's stories and comments, creates the sensation of a fairy tale or a science fiction novel, where the impossible becomes natural and all dreams come true.

But at that time I did not know all this, so after the brief glance at the book I switched my eyes to the chess board.

**Lev Aronin**
**David Bronstein**
Tartu 1962

position after 16.♗d1

My first feeling was that the position was very similar to those arising from the Open Ruy Lopez, with a perfect blocking knight on e6, a stable bishop defending the kingside

from g6 and a threatening central majority. In fact, things are better for Black here than in the Ruy Lopez, as his c-pawn is not blocked by the knight and White has a pawn on d3 instead of f2, thus sparing Black the danger of a majority kingside attack. As an experienced Open Variation player, I knew Black should prepare ...c7-c5 and/or ...f7-f6. As the former has been accomplished already, my first impulse was 16...♕d7, followed by ...♖ae8 and ...f7-f6/f5 soon, which would ensure a comfortable position. Instead of applause I heard: 'Where is your optimism? I would go 16...b5!' I tried to argue that, with almost all White's pieces ready for an attack, it would be a better idea to secure the kingside before launching a counter-attack, but when she opened the book we read:

**16...b5!** My first feeling was that the plan initiated by this move was too simplistic, something like a child's dream, an attack on the wing sustained by the beautiful bishop but without caring about the centre. I remembered that when I was five or six years old, I played a few games against myself with the 'opening' 1.e4 c5 2.♘f3 ♘c6 3.d4 c4?!?!, followed by ...b7-b5. At some point, I noticed this would just drop a pawn, but the dream of an early pawn queenside attack remained deep in my mind. The simplicity behind Black's plan is only apparent. Bronstein had needed to assess, not only his chances of queenside success (the easier part), but also his defensive resources. His 'optimism' was generated by deep understanding and not by superficiality.

**Mihail Marin and his wife Mariya Yugina in a selfie taken on the ferry from Sardinia, as they prepare to play through a Bronstein game.**

White's play in the next phase is also logical, aimed at exchanging the main kingside defenders.

**17.♘e2 c4 18.d4**

Consolidating e5 and preventing ...d5-d4.

**18...b4 19.c3**

**19...♕a5**

This reveals a hidden aspect concerning White's imperfect coordination. The a2-pawn has no defence. But the last move also allows White to develop his kingside initiative by weakening Black's control of the h4-d8-diagonal.

Nimzowitsch (and probably many other players, including myself) would consider 19...a5 more principled, since it prepares undermining the pawn chain from its base with ...a4-a3. Bronstein must have rejected it due to 20.♗a4, but actually Black's position is so strong that he could afford the spectacular 20...bxc3 21.bxc3 ♘b4! 22.cxb4 axb4, with similar compensation for the piece as later in the game. Objectively, Bronstein's move is also very strong, but it required a deep understanding of concrete strategic and dynamic nuances.

**20.♗h4! ♖ab8 21.♗xe7 ♘xe7**
**22.♘g5** The start of a thematic fight for the e6-square.

**22...♘c7** The main idea seems to be driving the enemy knight back with ...h7-h6 in order to retrieve possession of the blocking square. But in the end the knight will be reserved a different fate.

**23.♘f4 h6 24.♘xg6**

David Bronstein, as seen by Mariya Yugina, who is also an avid painter.

**24...fxg6!**

In the Open Ruy Lopez, this way of capturing is also thematic, but in this game it is absolutely forced, since 24...♘xg6? would allow 25.♗xf7! ♖xf7 26.♖xf7 ♔xf7 27.♗h5 ♕b6 28.♕c2, soon retrieving the piece with an advantage.

**25.♖xf8+ ♖xf8 26.cxb4 ♕xa2**
**27.♘f3** As a consequence of ...♕a5, the game has lost some of its strategic contours. Both players have weaknesses, which tends to make the play become concrete. I find this type of evolution typical for Bronstein's flexibility of mind.

**27...♘b5!?** After 16...b5 and 19...♕a5 this is the third move that apparently neglects the kingside defence and focuses mainly on the

other wing. For an Open Ruy Lopez player, 27...♘e6 would be an almost automatic answer, and quite a good one, too. But Bronstein's move creates the potential threat of ...c4-c3 without fearing the advance of the e-pawn, which would later be blocked by the other, passive knight.

**28.♕c2** White probably feared that after a neutral move like 28.h3, Black would break through with 28...♖xf3 (actually 28...♖b8 is also strong) 29.♗xf3 c3 30.♕c1 cxb2 31.♕b1 ♕b3 32.♖e2 ♘xd4 33.♖xb2 ♕e3, with excellent control and initiative for the exchange.

The last move avoids the pin, but weakens the e1-a5 diagonal. Hence:

**28...a5!?**

At first sight, this solves part of White's problems by ridding him of his double pawns. Besides, it allows White's next and apparently freeing move. Bronstein's attitude towards double pawns will be illustrated in the next example, and his more concrete move-by-move approach in this game proves right.

**29.♕a4!?**

Apparently solving all White's problems, as after 29...♕xa4 30.♗xa4 ♘c7 31.bxa5 ♖a8 32.b4 cxb3 33.♗xb3 he cannot be worse.

One important point is that after 29.bxa5 ♕xa5, White has no adequate defence against the threats ...♘xd4 and ...♖xf3. For instance: 30.♖g1 (30.♖e2 ♘xd4 and 30.♕e2 ♖f4 are equally hopeless) 30...♘f5, and the d4-pawn is doomed. A perfect illustration of White's poor coordination!

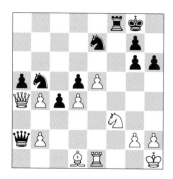

**29...♕xb2!!**
Together with the next move, the crowning of Black's aggressive plan, proving that Bronstein's strategic approach was both coherent and very concrete.
**30.♕xb5 ♕xb4! 31.♕xb4**
White cannot avoid the queen exchange, since 31.♕d7 is met by 31...♕xe1+!, and mate.
**31...axb4 32.♔g1**
Black has only two pawns for the piece and his kingside structure is imperfect. But White has utterly failed to improve his coordination and his bishop remains hopelessly useless. It is Bronstein's merit that he correctly evaluated this endgame as close to winning. Without giving concrete lines he complains, though, that, starting here, his play was far from optimal.

**32...b3?!** This prematurely exposes the b-pawn. Stronger was 32...♖a8 33.♔f1 ♖a2, with ...b5-b4 to follow soon.
**33.♔f2 g5 34.h3 ♖a8 35.g4?**
Missing his chance with 35.♘d2, planning the equalizing ♗xb3.
**35...♖a2+ 36.♔e3 ♘g6 37.♘d2**

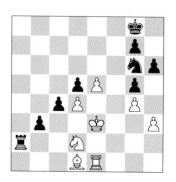

**37...♖a1**
Not a bad move, but this is the moment where Black misses a first clear win with 37...♘f4, threatening ...♘g2+: 38.♖g1 (controlling g2, as 38.♖h1 allows 38...♘g2+ 39.♔e2 c3, winning) 38...♖a1, followed by ...b3-b2 and ...c4-c3.
**38.♘f3 ♘f4** And now 38...b2 was simpler, as after 39.♗c2 Black has 39...♘h4!, when White's hanging pieces cannot stop the pawn.
Black eventually won after 30 more moves, but this is no longer related to our theme.

**Double pawns**
I was so impressed by this game that I immediately asked Mariya to show me an example related to one of Bronstein's specialties, the double pawns. I mainly knew the following simple combination, which did not entirely satisfy me.

**Vladas Mikenas**
**David Bronstein**
Tallinn 1965

position after 23.♗f3

According to Bronstein, double pawns imply an extra open file. In this position his opponent failed to notice that the a8-rook is taking active part in the play as he met **23...♕e5** with **24.♖b4??** There followed **24...♖xa3!** and due to the back rank weakness White resigned.

Following my request, it was not long before Mariya suggested the following game.

**David Bronstein**
**Isaac Boleslavsky**
Moscow match 1950 (7)

position after 20...♕e7

This was the seventh game of the 14-game (!) Candidates' playoff. Bronstein won by one point, thus qualifying for his famous match against Botvinnik.
The double-pawn issue will occur one move later, but I could not help starting from this position, as Bronstein's next move is truly remarkable.

'I was so impressed by this game that I immediately asked Mariya to show me an example related to one of Bronstein's specialties, the double pawns.'

David Bronstein and his good friend Isaac Boleslavsky preparing for the match against Botvinnik. Many years later, in 1984, Bronstein married Boleslavsky's daughter Tatiana.

At this level one might expect an instructive ending with a good bishop versus a bad one, and I was already asking myself whether my wife had understood what I had been asking for.

**21.♘xa6!!**

I was startled to see this move. Did Bronstein really exchange his good knight for the bad bishop? But then I understood that after, say, 21.♖fb1 ♗c4 the bishop would actually be more active than its rival on g2 (among other things, it ensures Black against c3-c4), while Black would be better prepared for a kingside attack with ...g7-g5.

After the exchange White's bishop will be more active than the knight, as the latter cannot get to e4 or c4 easily, while the former could add force to c3-c4 or simply go to b5, to undermine the blockade. This is a perfect illustration of the rule that it matters less which pieces you exchange – the main thing is which pieces are left on board!

I immediately remembered a couple of games played by Fischer two decades later on his way to the supreme title. In both cases, he

exchanged his dominant knight for Petrosian's supposedly bad bishop. After these games the American was highly praised for his flexibility in thinking and lack of preconceived ideas. Without diminishing his merits, we can notice that Bronstein displayed a similar approach much earlier (which reminded me of the voices that claimed that Fischer did not do much new or revolutionary, but mainly did what others had done before, only a lot better!)

**21...♖xa6**

**22.♕c5!!**

The second and biggest shock. White voluntarily spoils his structure, turning the knight into a seemingly perfect blocker.

After the natural 22.♖fb1 ♕xa3 23.♖xa3 ♖b6 24.♖b5 White retains some pressure, but unlike in the game, the black king could march all the way to d6, ensuring Black satisfactory stability. Apart from the aspect mentioned by Bronstein, double pawns may control essential squares more effectively than 'normal' ones.

**22...♖b8 23.♖fb1 ♕xc5 24.dxc5 ♔f8 25.♖b5 ♖aa8 26.♔f2 ♔e7 27.♔e3**

At this point in the game, Black is stable enough, but the knight's blockade is not 100 percent effective, since the c6-square can be attacked by the bishop. If White succeeds in playing ♗b5, the only way to defend the knight would be ...♔d7, leaving Black under a permanent pin, while the plan based on c3-c4 remains valid.

Bronstein writes that both opponents thought White was better here, but later he reached the conclusion that the position is just equal. Still, one way or another the play remains one-sided.

**27...♖g8 28.♖ab1**

Taking the rook out of the knight's range, since 28.c4?! ♘b4 29.cxd5? runs into 29...♘c2+.

**28...♖gb8**

Boleslavsky refrains from the initially intended 28...g5 which, according to Bronstein, could lead to the following variation: 29.fxg5 hxg5 30.c4 ♘b4 31.cxd5 ♘xd5+ (the point is that 31...exd5 runs into 32.♖1xb4 axb4 33.♗xd5, retrieving the exchange with an advantage in the rook ending) 32.♗xd5 exd5 33.♔d4, with a dangerous endgame for Black due to White's king activity.

**29.♔d3 ♔d7 30.e3 ♔e7 31.♔d2 ♖c8 32.♗f3 g6**

There was no tactical problem with 32...g5 already. If Black could play ...g5-g4, his fortress would most probably be unbreakable. But White can prevent this with 33.h3, when apart from his queenside worries Black should permanently reckon with g3-g4. If 33...♖g8 34.♔e2 gxf4 35.gxf4 ♖g3, White neutralizes the counterattack with 36.♔f2, when the h3-pawn is taboo due to ♔g3, trapping the rook, while 36...♖ag8?! loses an exchange to 37.♗g4!.

**33.♗e2 h5**

Played with the obvious intention of ridding himself of the h-pawn if White opens the kingside.

**34.h3 ♖g8 35.♖b7**

**35...♖gc8** Due to the c5-pawn, this is the only reasonable way of defending c7, keeping Black passive. The pin after 35...♔d7 36.♗b5 is in all probability decisive, while after 35...♖ac8 36.♖1b6 the seventh-

rank pin would soon cost Black the a-pawn. In both lines the impossibility of playing ...♔d6 restricts Black's defensive resources.

**36.g4**

With no obvious queenside progress in view, White opens a new front.

**36...hxg4 37.hxg4 ♘d8**

Boleslavsky intends to take measures against the intrusion along the h-file. The alternative was 37...♖ab8, trying to keep White busy on the queenside or else free his c8-rook (after ♖7b5). But leaving a6 undefended could be exploited with 38.gxf5 gxf5 39.♖1b6, planning ♗a6, with the probable gain of the a-pawn. And if 39...♔f6, unpinning the c-pawn then 40.♖xb8 ♘xb8 41.♖b5 ♘c6 42.♖b7, followed by ♗a6, ♖b5 and ♗b7, with similar consequences.

**38.♖7b2 ♘f7 39.g5**

**39...♔d7 40.c4!**

After this long-awaited break Black's fortress will soon crumble.

**40...dxc4 41.♗f3!** For the time being, the bishop is needed on this diagonal to spoil Black's coordina-

tion. This is once again an illustration of Bronstein's flexibility of mind.

**41...♖a7** In case of 41...c6 42.♖b7+ ♖c7 43.♖1b6 ♘d8 44.♖xc7+ ♔xc7 45.♔c3, the endgame remains very promising for White. One important aspect is that 45...♖b8? allows 46.♖xb8 ♔xb8 47.♗h5!.

**42.♔c3 c6 43.♖h2 ♔e7 44.♗e2 ♔f8 45.♗xc4 ♖e8 46.♖b6 ♖c7 47.♖a6**

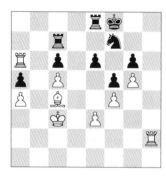

White wins the a-pawn while retaining his domination, and Bronstein won 20 moves later.

If compared to the previous game, this one looks almost eventless, but the exchange on a6 and the creation of double pawns make it a strategic jewel.

## Botvinnik, of course

There has been a lot of discussion around the central event of Bronstein's career, his match against Botvinnik. The World Champion's fans shared the view that he was in poor form, and even though he managed to refute many of Bron-

# COMPLETE YOUR COLLECTION!

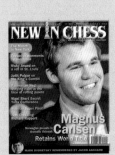

stein's experiments, he frequently spoiled games somewhere before the time-control.

During a 24-game match a lot happens and Bronstein, too, complained about missing several favourable opportunities. But speaking about experiments, the 17th game features an original innovation which has not only successfully stood the test of time, but also contained a small psychological trap.

### Mikhail Botvinnik
### David Bronstein
Moscow match 1951 (17)
Nimzo-Indian Defence, Rubinstein Variation

**1.d4 ♘f6 2.c4 e6 3.♘c3 ♗b4 4.e3 b6 5.♘ge2 ♗a6!?**
Over the decades, this has turned into one of the main lines of the 4...b6 systems, but at that time it was a complete novelty.
**6.a3 ♗e7 7.♘g3 d5 8.cxd5 ♗xf1 9.♘xf1 exd5**

We have reached a hybrid of the Carlsbad structure in which, due to Bronstein's novelty, Black has exchanged his potentially bad bishop. True, ...b7-b6 counts as a slight weakness, but if Black refrains from ...c7-c5, White's queenside attacking chances are slim. Besides, Bronstein must have intuitively felt that, as a former Sämisch Attack specialist (it is enough to remember his win over Capablanca), Botvinnik would try to advance his central majority in order to activate his remaining bishop (which in the Carlsbad structure stands on f4 or g5).

When experimenting in the opening,

Bronstein surely took into account not only his opponent's repertoire, but also his way of handling the related structures in general.
**10.♘g3 ♕d7 11.♕f3 ♘c6 12.0-0**
If 12.♘f5 ♗f8 13.0-0 g6 the knight retreat would transpose to the game, while the tactical attempt 14.e4 does not yield anything concrete: 14...dxe4 (only not 14...gxf5 15.exd5 ♘xd4 16.♕e3+ with a strong initiative) 15.♘xe4 ♘xe4 16.♕xe4+ ♕e6 17.♘d6+ ♔d7!, and after the forced queen swap the attack is over.
**12...g6**

**13.♗d2** Now and later the plan based on b2-b4 would have made sense. Botvinnik must have disliked weakening the light squares (actually

### 'There has been a lot of discussion around the central event of Bronstein's career, his match against Botvinnik.'

his later a3-a4 proves this), but the way he regroups in order to prepare e3-e4 is not effective.
**13...0-0 14.♘ce2 h5 15.♖fc1 h4 16.♘f1 ♘e4 17.♘f4 a5 18.♖c2 ♗d8 19.♗e1 ♘e7 20.♕e2 ♘d6**
Black's regrouping is far more to the point. The knight on d6 inhibits both e3-e4 and b2-b4 (the latter would allow installing a permanent knight on c4), the bishop defends Black's only weakness and the reserve knight's plan will be revealed after the next move.
**21.f3 g5 22.♘d3 ♕e6 23.a4 ♘g6 24.h3 f5 25.♗c3 ♗f6 26.♖e1 ♖ae8 27.♕d1 ♖f7 28.b3 ♖fe7 29.♗b2**
Even now, 29.b4 axb4 30.♗xb4 might still have offered defensive chances.

**The opening ceremony of the 1951 world title match between Mikhail Botvinnik (far left) and David Bronstein (far right). In the middle FIDE President Folke Rogard.**

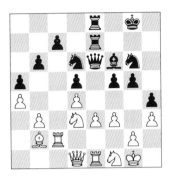

**29...f4!** This heralds the complete fiasco of White's middlegame play. By failing to carry out his favourite central break, he turned his central majority into a weakness.

**30.♘e5** 30.exf4 allows 30...♛xe1 31.♘xe1 ♖xe1, followed by ...♘xf4, with a decisive attack. Botvinnik played the next moves very quickly as if he wanted to get rid of the game.

**30...♗xe5 31.dxe5 ♘f7 32.exf4 ♘xf4 33.♘h2 c5 34.♘g4 d4 35.♘f6+? ♛xf6** White resigned.

I will round off with a short fragment that will once again makes us feel the strength of the doubled pawns.

**Lubomir Kavalek
David Bronstein**
Szombathely 1966

position after 13...c5

If examined from a purely structural point of view, Black's central pawn structure could not have been worse, since the f5-square is weak and the pawn on f6 immobilizes its backward colleague. Optimally, Black should play ...f5-f4 and possibly ...f7-f6. Even ...f6-f5, followed by ...e5-e4, would be an improvement, since the pawns

would offer some breathing space for the pieces.

White's next move does not seem to give him the time for any of this.

**14.h4** The point is that the bishop on g6 is tightly integrated in the structure, mending all the weaknesses by defending f5 and connecting the pawns on h7 and f7. If Black is forced to look for a way to save his bishop, White would most likely find a way to establish a blockade on f5.

**14...f5!!** Bronstein immediately starts improving his structure, without caring about the 'tall pawn' on g6.

**15.f4** If 15.h5 e4, White would probably have to play 16.f4, transposing to the game, since 16.hxg6 hxg6 would offer Black a decisive attack along the h-file.

**15...e4 16.h5 f6 17.g3?!**
17.hxg6 hxg6 18.♗g7 ♖h7 retrieves the bishop, but White would have done better to avoid this weakening move.

**17...0-0-0 18.♖f2 ♗e8**

The position has changed dramatically over the past few moves. By advancing his pawns White has chronically weakened his g-file,

'He looked, indeed, like a sorcerer, performing little miracles that others could or would not have the courage and imagination to find.'

which is available to Black precisely because of the doubled pawns. The pawns control g4 and g5, thus immobilizing White's structure and bishop. Play one-sidedly favours Black, and Bronstein won after a long fight marked by some inaccuracies on both sides.

**Conclusion**

Bronstein's deep understanding gave him the ability to carry out apparently simple plans conceived by his mind and heart. He also had a marked flexibility in thinking, a talent for adapting his plan move by move, according to small tactical and static nuances, leaving the false impression of a lack of coherence in the process, but proving logical overall when everything was were done. He looked, indeed, like a sorcerer, performing little miracles that others could or would not have the courage and imagination to find.

Here are a few practical pieces of advice that can be inferred from Bronstein's games:

1. Do not shy away from generating ambitious, grandiose plans! They may be achievable!
2. While pursuing a global plan is generally desirable, feel free to adapt it to concrete circumstances!
3. Do your best to understand the pawn structure's static and dynamic essence in depth! Doubled pawns control important squares and leave the neighbouring files open. This is more than just a cliché. ∎

**1. Lagno-Karavade**
Astana 2019

The careless 38...♖c1-c2? allowed **39.♖xh6+!** and Black resigned in view of 39...gxh6 40.♕f6+ ♔h7 41.♕xf7+ ♔h8 42.♘g6 mate.

**2. Barsegyan-Höfelsauer**
Austria 2019

**45.♖d6!** ♘e3 45...♖xd6 46.♘xd6+ ♔f4 47.♘e6/47.♘g6 mate. **46.♖xf6+!** Or 46.♖xd5+!. **46...♘xf6 47.♘d6+ ♔f4 48.♘e6** (or 48.♘g6) mate.

**3. Ivic-Gledura**
Skopje 2019

**37...♕e7! 38.♕d3 ♖xe2!** 38...♕g5+? 39.♖g3 ♖xe2 40.♕xb4+. **39.♕d1!?** ♕f6 39...♕g5+ 40.♖g3 ♖d2! wins too. **40.♔f3 ♖e1+!** White resigned.

**4. Asadli-M.Popov**
Moscow 2019

**22...♗c2!** Exploiting the pins. **23.♖xc2 ♖xd4! 24.♕e2 ♖e4!** The killer. **25.♕d3** Or 25.♔f2 ♖xf4+ and White collapses. **25...♘xc2+** Double check! **26.♔f2 ♕c5+ 27.♔g3 ♖e1 28.♕xc2 ♘e3** White resigned.

**5. Artemiev-Hracek**
Skopje 2019

**25.♖xg7! ♔xg7 26.♖g3+ ♔h8 27.♘xd5! ♖xd5 28.♗h6 ♘f6** The point is seen after 28...♖g8 29.♖xg8+ ♔xg8 30.♕g4+. **29.♕xf6+!** And Black resigned in view of 29...♘xf6 30.♗g7+ ♔g8 31.♗xf6 mate.

**6. Smirin-Sidorenko**
Israel 2019

**32.g6! fxg6** 32...♖xg6 33.♖h8+; 32...♖d8 33.♕b6. **33.♖h7! ♕xh7 34.♕xe6+ ♔f8 35.♕xc8+ ♗e8 36.♖e1** Black resigned as after 36...♖d7 37.♕c5+ ♔f7 38.f4 followed by 39.♗d5+ he loses the queen.

**7. Potapov-Kryakvin**
Moscow 2019

**56...♖b4!** Threatening the bishop (57.♖xa2 ♗c4+) and trying to deflect it (57.♖xb4 f2), as well as cutting off the white king. **57.h5+** 57.d7 ♗xd7 doesn't change anything. **57...♔xh5 58.♔d2 ♗a4 59.♖a5 ♔g6** White resigned.

**8. Ofitserian-Gaifullin**
Moscow 2019

Strongest was **30...♗xf2+ 31.♔xf2 ♘e5! 32.♖xd8+ ♖xd8 33.♗xd8 ♕d2+ 34.♔g1 ♕e3+ 35.♔g2** 35.♔f1 ♘d3 36.♗b6 ♗h3+ 37.♔g2 ♕xf3+. **35...♕xf3+ 36.♔g1 ♕e3+ 37.♔g2 ♕e2+ 38.♔g1 ♗h3 39.♗b6 ♕g4!** mating.

**9. Anton-Soysal**
Skopje 2019

Black could have launched a decisive attack by **24...♘f3+! 25.♗xf3** 25.♔h1 ♕f4. **25...♖xh3 26.♗g2** 26.♔g2 ♕f4! 27.♕xd8+ also doesn't hold. **26...♖g3! 27.♖fe1 ♖xg2+! 28.♔xg2 ♕xg4+ 29.♔f1 ♖h8 30.♕xc5+ ♔d7!** and wins.

LARS O.A. HEDLUND

SIGEMAN & Co

**A quarter of a century of top chess in Malmö**

# No one keeps up with Jones

Gawain Jones once again proved that he's become a consistent 2700-player, as the Englishman deservedly won the jubilee edition of the TePe Sigeman tournament. **NILS GRANDELIUS** reports.

This year's TePe Sigeman tournament was the 25th edition of the event in Malmö, and the third time law firm Sigeman & Co teamed up with TePe, Sweden's leading manufacturer of dental products. The anniversary edition saw a couple of changes, most notably the move from the classical – but somewhat old – Hipp Theatre to the ultra-modern event centre Malmö Live, and the increase of the number of participants from six to eight.

The change of venue meant perhaps slightly less colourful images, but also a technical boost. For instance, the internet connection was said to be 500(!) times faster than at the Hipp, which certainly also boosted the popularity of the live broadcast.

An unexpected problem that came with playing at Malmö Live manifested itself in the first round, when reigning World Junior Champion Parham Maghsoodloo arrived late for his game after getting lost in the labyrinthine corridors of the impressive building.

**A big fight**

As usual, the field was composed of some international stars known for their fighting spirit, some new young hopes, the local hero (Tiger Hillarp Persson lives in Malmö – ed.) and myself. As the top seed and fresh from an impressive performance in Shenzhen (see elsewhere in this issue), Pentala Harikrishna was considered the pre-tournament favourite. However, the first round already showed where things were heading. While Harikrishna did not manage to break through Tiger Hillarp Persson's Caro-Kann Defence, second seed and fresh 2700-club member Gawain Jones was engaged in a big fight with Maghsoodloo.

NOTES BY
**Gawain Jones**

**Parham Maghsoodloo**
**Gawain Jones**
Malmö 2019 (1)
English Opening, Symmetrical Variation

The following game was played in the first round. My opponent arrived a little late, after having got lost trying to find the playing venue. I think nerves affected his play, as he spent far longer than normal on the opening moves.
**1.♘f3 ♘f6 2.c4 c5 3.b3!?**
Offbeat but also quite topical.
**3...g6 4.♗b2 ♗g7 5.g3 0-0 6.♗g2 d6**

**7.d4**
If White were to castle, 7.0-0, then the intention was to play against the b2-bishop with 7...e5. This is a position that's had quite a lot of outings in games between elite players at faster time-controls.
**7...d5!?**
It makes a strange impression to play ...d7-d5 in two moves rather than one, but it's in Black's interest that White has committed to d2-d4. The centre is very fluid and Black can try to exploit the pin down the a1-h8 diagonal on the vulnerable bishop on b2.
We've now transposed to a Double

Fianchetto against the King's Indian or Grünfeld.
**8.dxc5 dxc4 9.♘bd2 ♘a6 10.0-0 ♘xc5 11.♘xc4 ♗e6**

**12.♕c1**
A good move, but Parham had already spent in excess of an hour to reach this position, and the later time-trouble cost him dearly.
I've actually had this position before via a different move order. In a rapid game from the British Knockout, I faced 12.♖c1, but this allows 12...♗h6!, when the rook is rather short on squares. My opponent David Howell couldn't find anything better than 13.♖a1 (½-½, 25, Howell-Jones, London 2018).
**12...♖c8 13.♖d1 ♕e8 14.♕f4**
Here's where I had my first long think of the game. Despite the fairly symmetrical nature of the position, there are a lot of tactics bubbling below the surface.

**14...♘ce4** I considered 14...♘a4 for a while, but wasn't happy with Black's position after 15.♗xf6 ♗xf6 16.♘d6! exd6 17.♕xf6 ♘c3 18.♖e1.
Perhaps 14...♗xc4! was the most accurate: 15.♕xc4 (this is the preferable recapture from a structural point of view, but White has some problems with the loose bishop on b2. 15.bxc4 is possible, of course, but Black will get good play on the queenside) 15...♘ce4 16.♕d4 (16.♕d3? ♘xf2! 17.♔xf2 ♘g4+, and the bishop falls) 16...♖c2, with strong counterplay.
**15.♘fe5 b5** The chaos starts!

**16.♘a5 ♖c2** After 16...♘c3 17.♗xc3 ♖xc3 18.♘ec6 is unpleasant; my queenside is too vulnerable.
**17.♗d4 ♗d5 18.♕e3 ♕a8**

**19.♗h3?!** Afterwards Parham was very critical of this. It's more accurate for White to start with 19.f3! ♘d6, and only then 20.♗h3, cutting out the option I used in the game.
**19...h6! 20.♖dc1 ♘g5?!**
Parham was already down to just increments to reach move 40, so I wanted to keep the game as complicated as possible. Objectively, though, the move is dubious.

'**My opponent arrived a little late, after having got lost trying to find the playing venue.**'

**21.♗f1** I think very few players would take the material on offer here without enough time to calculate the consequences, but he could have played 21.♖xc2! ♘xh3+ 22.♔f1 ♗xb3 23.♖c6. White isn't mated immediately, but Black has a pawn for the exchange and after 23...♗d5

ANALYSIS DIAGRAM

White has to be certain that there won't be a terminal discovery with the bishop, followed by ...♕h1#.
In the press conference afterwards, we didn't see a kill after 24.♖a6?!, but 24...♗g2+ 25.♔e1 ♕c8! 26.♖xa7 ♘d5 is pretty dangerous.
24.♖cc1? ♘g4! highlights the danger in White's position: 25.♘xg4 ♗c4 (oddly, he can't fight for control of the long diagonal) 26.♔e1 (26.f3 ♗xd4 27.♕xd4 ♕xf3+) 26...♗xd4 27.♕xd4 ♖d8, and due to the threat of ...♕h1+ White has to give up his queen.
Unfortunately, the engine pours cold water on my idea, with its suggestion of 24.♖ac1! ♗xc6 25.♘axc6. Despite the pawn deficit, White is doing very well here, as he has such better coordination.
**21...♖fc8 22.♖xc2 ♖xc2 23.♖c1 ♕c8 24.♘ac6?**

The after-party at the Sigeman office before bughouse took over: Parham Maghsoodloo, Tiger Hillarp-Persson, Gawain Jones, Pentala Harikrishna and (half visible) Nihal Sarin.

I was expecting this as, short on time, it looks like Black might have just blundered.

**24...♖xc1?!**
This was my idea; but I'd missed something much stronger.
I didn't see a kill after 24...♘h3+ 25.♗xh3 ♕xh3 26.f3 (26.♘xe7+ ♔h7 27.♘xd5 ♘xd5, and White has to give up his queen), but here Black has the beautiful 26...♘g4! 27.♘xg4 ♗xf3! (the move I'd overlooked. White is overloaded) 28.exf3 (28.♕xf3 ♖xc1+) 28...♕g2, mate.
**25.♕xc1** White can't win my queen: 25.♘xe7+? ♔h7 26.♘xc8 ♘h3, mate.
**25...♔h7**

**26.f3?**
Now White gets too tangled up in the pins. 26.♕c5! was necessary.
**26...♘d7 27.♕c3 ♘e6**

**28.♘xe7?!** Taking the pawn is tempting, but now White drops a piece.

28.♘b4 was his last chance, but it's still quite miserable. Black can choose between retaining the pressure with 28...♗b7 or cashing in with 28...♕xc3 29.♗xc3 ♗xb3!, when White will be a pawn down whichever piece he takes.

**28...♕b7** Now there's no defence to either ...♘xe5 or ...♘xd4.

**29.f4**

29.e4 ♘xd4 30.♕xd4 ♘xe5 31.♘xd5 ♘xf3+ is one problem.

**29...♘xe5 30.♘xd5 ♘xd4 31.e4**

So Black is a whole piece up for a pawn. My technique to reach the time-control was woeful, perhaps due to a combination of first-round nerves and slipping into time-trouble. Luckily, I didn't quite put the win in jeopardy.

**31...♘ec6** 31...♘g4 32.♕c5 (32.♕c1 f5) 32...♕a6 33.a4 ♕e6! was the simplest of the many wins available.

**32.♔h1 ♘e7 33.♕c7 ♕xc7 34.♘xc7**

With the queens off the board it should be simple, but White does have annoying light-square control.

**34...b4 35.♗c4 ♔g8** I can't really explain why I didn't start with 35...f5.

**36.♔g2 g5 37.♔f2 ♘g6 38.♘d5 a5 39.e5 ♔f8 40.♔e3 ♘c6**

Time-control reached, and now some work to do to convert the win, but luckily, with a pause I could regroup and start playing sensibly again.

**41.♔e4 h5 42.♗b5 ♘ce7 43.♗b6 gxf4 44.♘d7+ ♔g8 45.gxf4 ♘f8 46.♘c5 ♘e6 47.♘d3 ♗h6 48.h4 ♔g7 49.♗c4** 49.f5 is met by 49...♘xf5! 50.♔xf5 ♘d4+. **49...♔g6**

Black's pieces are coordinated again and the rest is easy.

**50.♗xe6 fxe6 51.♘c5 ♔f7 52.♘b7 ♘d5 53.♘d6+ ♔e7 54.f5 ♘c3+ 55.♔d3 ♗f4 56.f6+ ♔d7 57.♔d4 ♗g3 58.♘b7 ♗f2+ 59.♔d3 ♘xa2 60.♘xa5 ♗xh4 61.♘b7** White resigned.

∎ ∎ ∎

In that same round, 14-year-old Indian prodigy Nihal Sarin played a very nice positional game against former European Champion Ivan Saric, but stumbled in the end.

**Nihal Sarin**
**Ivan Saric**
Malmö 2019 (1)

position after 66...♖f6

White is obviously winning with queen against rook, but here Sarin fell into Saric's last trick:

**67.♕a6+?? ♔c2!**

And suddenly the threat of ...♖xd6, combined with the advance of the b-pawn, is enough for Black to escape.

**68.♕c4**

68.♔g2 ♖g6+ 69.♔h1 would save the knight, but 69...b3 would even force

Nihal Sarin got a winning position against Ivan Saric, but a brief concentration lapse cost the Indian youngster half a point.

White to find 70.♕b6! in order not to lose.

**68...♖xd6 69.♕xb4 ♖d4 70.♕b7 g5** And a draw was agreed a few moves later... (½-½, 77)

That was a tragic turn of events for the young Indian, but also surely a good lesson of just how important it is to keep maximum concentration until the game is over. Such saves can often be the start of a glorious tournament, but for Saric it turned out to be a sign of very bad form. After losing his next game to Hillarp Persson he didn't manage to find back his footing and ended up not winning a single game for the first time in a very long time.

### Trademark fashion

In Round 3, Pentala Harikrishna joined Gawain Jones in the lead when he beat me in his trademark fashion.

**Nils Grandelius**
**Pentala Harikrishna**
Malmö 2019 (3)

position after 19...♕xa8

A typical Italian has led to a normal position in which White is a tiny bit better but Black is very solid. During the game, I thought I spotted a nice way of increasing my advantage, and fell for a deep positional trick.

**20.dxe5 dxe5 21.♗xb6 cxb6 22.♘h5**

This is the idea. As d7 is hanging, I am able to force a doubling of the f-pawns, after which I'm better on both sides of the board, I thought. Then Harikrishna confidently played:

**22...♗e6 23.♘xf6+ gxf6**

And I realized that my former optimism wasn't very well-founded. It is true that my structure looks nicer, but a few small but important dynamic factors work in Black's favour: the bishop on e6 is stronger than its counterpart, the g6-knight has access to the f4-square, and my knight is slightly misplaced.
But the main problem for me is that Black's counterplay on the queenside is very fast. An interesting point was made by Harikrishna after the

yet to give up all my winning hopes.
**24...♕a2 25.♕b1**
After 25.♕c1, 25...b4 gives nice counterplay.
**25...♕xb1 26.♖xb1 b4**
OK, I didn't manage to achieve anything in this game; time to make a draw and go home, I thought. Precisely the moment when Harikrishna is at his strongest!

**27.cxb4?**
27.♘g4! ♗xg4 28.hxg4 ♖c8 29.♗b3 bxc3 30.bxc3 ♖xc3 31.♗d5 was the

## 'Time to make a draw and go home, I thought. Precisely the moment when Harikrishna is at his strongest!'

game: if we undouble Black's pawns by moving b5 to c7, then White would indeed be a bit better, as the counterplay is much slower!

**24.♘h2?!**
24.♗b3 was one emergency break: 24...♖d8 25.♕c2 ♗xb3 26.♕xb3 ♕a4 27.♕xa4 bxa4, with a very drawish endgame. But I wasn't entirely ready

safest way, with an immediate draw.
**27...♖c8 28.♗d3 ♖d8 29.♗f1 ♖d4!**

After a few careless moves, Black has completely taken over. Now I started fighting again, but Harikrishna showed excellent technique and convincingly won the game some 40 moves later... (0-1, 72)

In a tournament with only seven rounds, this basically meant the end of my winning ambitions, and the second half became a race between the two 2700-players. They both ground down their opponents in long endgames in Round 4 and drew promising positions in Round 5. Then, in Round 6, Gawain Jones punished Tiger Hillarp Persson's dubious play in exemplary fashion.

**Tiger Hillarp Persson**
**Gawain Jones**
Malmö 2019 (6)

position after 20...♖be8

White has sacrificed a pawn, but with his last move Black has invited him to take it back. Tiger, who did not have too much time left, thought for a few minutes and decided to try his luck.

**21.♘xd4 ♘xd4 22.♗xd4 ♗xd4 23.♖xd4 f5**

**24.♖xd6**
The only move, but Jones had calculated quite a bit further.
24.♘f6+ ♖xf6 25.♖xe8+ ♕xe8 26.♗xb7 ♕e1+ 27.♔g2 f4! would be complete curtains.
**24...♕xd6! 25.♘xd6 ♖xe1+ 26.♗f1 ♘e5!**

**27.c5+** After 27.♘xb7 ♘f3+ 28.♔g2 ♖xf1 wins immediately, due to the fork on d2.
**27...♔h7 28.f4 ♘f3+ 29.♔f2**

**29...♖xf1+** The point, and what Tiger had needed to see in order not to take on d4 on move 21.
**30.♔e3 ♖e1+ 31.♔f2 ♖e2+**
White resigned. Very efficient play by Jones!

This meant that Jones had a half-point lead before the final round against Harikrishna. That final clash never really got exciting, since after building up a nice advantage Jones offered a draw on move 21, which was accepted. A well-deserved tournament victory for Jones, who has established himself as a consistent 2700-player.

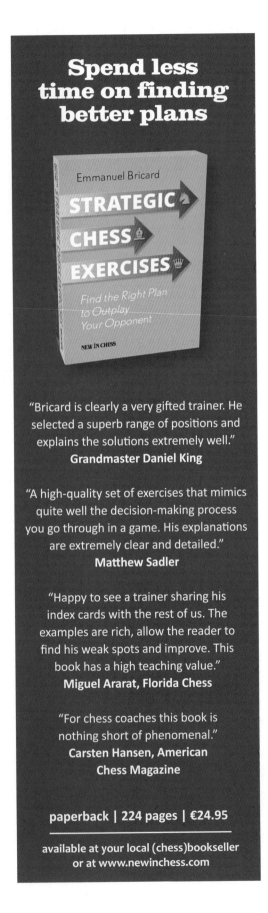
## Sometimes too predictable

Last place was shared between Ivan Saric and Tiger Hillarp Persson. Tiger had a lot of very interesting games. Not only did he face strong opposition, but he also challenged himself by playing the same dubious Sicilian in three black games in a row! The knowledge and understanding is certainly there, but not having enough tournaments at this level meant that decisions took a bit longer than usual, resulting in some unpleasant opening surprises and time-troubles.

Liviu-Dieter Nisipeanu's seven draws do not at all reflect his games. He could easily have been the player with the most decisive results, after being lost against Jones and Saric, while having a clear extra pawn against both Sarin and Maghsoodloo. To me it's simply a mystery how such a great fighter can play so many draws.

For the youngsters Parham Maghsoodloo and Nihal Sarin, playing in a strong round-robin was another good experience. On the first days, Maghsoodloo was a bit nervous, but towards the end he was clearly enjoying himself and was always a great entertainer in the commentary room. Sarin's style is more positional and stable, but where Maghsoodloo is completely unpredictable, Sarin can sometimes be a bit too predictable, as in his game against me.

**Nils Grandelius**
**Nihal Sarin**
Malmö 2019 (6)
Sicilian Defence, Rossolimo Variation

**1.e4!? c5!?**
The two first moves don't normally require a lot of comment, but here I think it's quite interesting. In a closed tournament it normally makes a lot of sense to try and be a bit less predictable, but I played 1.e4 in all my games, to which Nihal Sarin invariably replied 1...c5, followed by 2...♘c6. Risky, one would assume, but also following the example of our current World Champion!

**2.♘f3 ♘c6 3.♗b5 g6 4.0-0**
4.♗xc6 dxc6 5.d3 is the main line, and what Maghsoodloo tried against me two days earlier, but I was happy with my position in that game and decided to give the nowadays slightly less common 4.0-0 a try.

**4...♗g7 5.♖e1 ♘f6**
5...e5 is the main option, and was seen in Game 5 of Caruana-Carlsen, which continued 6.b4 ♘xb4 7.♗b2 a6 8.a3 axb5 9.axb4 ♖xa1 10.♗xa1 d6 11.bxc5 ♘e7, with sharp play.

**6.e5 ♘d5 7.♘c3 ♘c7 8.♗xc6 dxc6 9.♘e4**

**9...b6!?**
9...♘e6 is a calmer approach, after which 10.d3 0-0 11.♗e3 b6 12.♕d2 ♘d4 13.♘xd4 cxd4 14.♗h6 leads to quieter positions. Black is solid, but White argues that Black lacks a good plan and can try to put some pressure on the kingside.

**10.♘f6+**
10.d3 is a calmer but less critical approach.

**10...♔f8 11.♘e4 ♗g4**
11...h6 has been played a fair bit, but compared to 10.d3, White now has a dream version.

**12.d3**

## 12...♘e6

12...♗xe5 was the spectacular game Mamedov-Dubov (European Teams 2017), which continued 13.♘xe5! ♗xd1 14.♗h6+ ♔g8 15.♘xc6 ♗c2 (15...♕e8 16.♘f6+ exf6 17.♘e7+ ♕xe7 18.♖xe7 is very good for White) 16.♘xd8 ♖xd8 17.♘xc5 bxc5 18.♖xe7 ♘e6, with a strange position in which White is a piece down, but Black is stuck with his king and rook on h8. Practically speaking, White should do very well, and Mamedov duly won in convincing fashion.

## 13.♘eg5! ♘xg5 14.♗xg5 ♕d5!

Slower moves such as 14...h6 would lead to a grim defence after something like 15.♗f4 ♔g8 16.h3 ♗e6 17.♕e2, when White can choose between playing for the d4 break or regrouping the light pieces and trying to push f4-f5. Meanwhile, Black has the eternal problem of lacking a good plan.

## 15.♖e4!

15.a4 was actually the move I had intended before the game, showing some clear laziness during prep. During the game it didn't take me long to realize that the endgame after 15...♗xf3 16.♕xf3 ♕xf3 17.gxf3 a5 would be just fine for Black, despite the computer's favourable assessment for White. Adding the fact that my opponent had spent quite some time up to here, I decided to give the sharper try a go.

## 15...♗xf3

15...♗f5 can be played, but isn't fundamentally different from the other slower options. Black is solid, but White is better!

## 16.♕xf3 ♗xe5 17.♕e3

## 17...f6?

17...♗xb2! 18.c4 ♕f5 was the reason I thought 15.a4 made some sense. However, in spite of the fact that it's objectively holding for Black, it sure seems no fun to be unprepared and have to deal with something like 19.♗h6+ ♔g7 20.♖e1 ♕h5 21.♗f4.

## 18.♖e1! ♖e8

Nils Grandelius played 1.e4 in all his white games and proved excellently prepared in the popular Rossolimo Sicilian when he faced Nihal Sarin's current favourite defence.

18...h5 was what I considered the main try during the game, but 19.♗h6+ ♔g8 20.♗f4 looked promising, and indeed it is: 20...♗xf4 21.♕xf4 ♕d6 22.♕xd6 exd6 23.♖e6 ♔g7 24.♖xd6 ♖he8 25.♔f1. This is probably just lost for Black.

## 19.♗h6+ ♔g8

After 19...♔f7 20.♗f4 is the idea – now e7 hangs with check and Black is busted.

## 'Where Maghsoodloo is completely unpredictable, Sarin can sometimes be a bit too predictable.'

**20.c3?**

20.h3 was my main alternative during the game, the point being 20...♗d6 (20...e6 also annoyed me) 21.c4 ♕f5 22.g4 ♕d7 23.♖e6, and now, if 23...♗e5 24.♖xe5, the g4-pawn isn't hanging! Still, it didn't seem entirely clear to me after 23...♔f7, when it's not easy to see what my next move should be.

I completely failed to appreciate the value of the strongest move: 20.♕f3!. In fact, it's just completely winning for White. The point is that Black can never ever free himself. After 20...♗d6 (I thought 20...♔f7 21.♖xe5 ♕xf3 wouldn't work for me. However, the simple 21.c4 wins on the spot) 21.g4!! is the brilliant idea. 21...f5 (21...♔f7 22.c4 traps the queen) 22.gxf5 ♕xf5 23.♖1e3 ♕xf3 24.♖xf3.

**ANALYSIS DIAGRAM**

This doesn't help – Black still can never get out.

**20...♗d6**

20...e6? 21.d4 was the point of 20.c3.

**21.c4?!** Clearly showing that I am losing the thread of the game.
I should have played 21.g4! e5 22.f4,

and somewhat surprisingly, White is still doing well: 22...♔f7 23.c4 ♕e6 24.♕f3.

**21...♕h5!?** Nihal senses that I am completely drifting and starts playing for a win himself!
21...♕f5 22.g4 ♕d7 was also fine, as 23.♖e6 ♗e5 24.♖xe5 fxe5 25.♕xe5 ♕xg4+ 26.♔h1 ♕f3+ 27.♔g1 is just a perpetual.
**22.h4** Objectively the strongest move was 22.h3, with the crazy point 22...g5 23.♖h4! gxh4 24.♕e6+ ♕f7 25.♕g4+, with a perpetual.

**22...♗e5??**

A great pity; just when Black was starting to take over.

22...♔f7! was good for Black, as ...e5 is coming next. If I could just get rid of my rook on e4, I would have mate on e6, but there are no good squares!
**23.♗g5!**
Now I am just winning, as the queen gets trapped.
**23...♗d4 24.♖xd4 fxg5**
24...cxd4 25.♕e6+ ♔g7 26.g4 wins easily.
**25.♖d7 ♔g7 26.♖xe7+ ♖xe7 27.♕xe7+ ♔h6 28.♖e5**

**28...♕d1+**
28...♕xh4 loses to 29.♖e3.
**29.♔h2 ♕h5 30.♕xg5+**
Not the fastest, but the safest!
**30...♕xg5 31.hxg5+**

Now 31...♔g7 32.♖e7+ is a dead lost endgame, and 31...♔h5 32.♖h3 is just mate, so Black resigned.

The closing dinner made me even more convinced about the bright future of the two youngsters. Hardly taking time to eat, they were all blitz and bullet – their love for chess is simply endless. But after letting them throw pieces around for some time we switched to bughouse, and there the old guard still has a lot to say ☺. ∎

| Malmö 2019 | | | | | 1 | 2 | 3 | 4 | 5 | 6 | 7 | 8 | | TPR | cat. XVII |
|---|---|---|---|---|---|---|---|---|---|---|---|---|---|---|---|
| 1 | Gawain Jones | IGM | ENG | 2702 | * | ½ | ½ | ½ | 1 | ½ | 1 | 1 | 5 | 2816 |
| 2 | Pentala Harikrishna | IGM | IND | 2730 | ½ | * | 1 | ½ | ½ | 1 | ½ | ½ | 4½ | 2756 |
| 3 | Nils Grandelius | IGM | SWE | 2688 | ½ | 0 | * | ½ | ½ | 1 | ½ | 1 | 4 | 2710 |
| 4 | Liviu-Dieter Nisipeanu | IGM | GER | 2667 | ½ | ½ | ½ | * | ½ | ½ | ½ | ½ | 3½ | 2663 |
| 5 | Parham Maghsoodloo | IGM | IRI | 2671 | 0 | ½ | ½ | ½ | * | 0 | ½ | 1 | 3 | 2613 |
| 6 | Nihal Sarin | IGM | IND | 2598 | ½ | 0 | 0 | ½ | 1 | * | ½ | ½ | 3 | 2623 |
| 7 | Ivan Saric | IGM | CRO | 2694 | 0 | ½ | ½ | ½ | ½ | ½ | * | 0 | 2½ | 2557 |
| 8 | Tiger Hillarp Persson | IGM | SWE | 2563 | 0 | ½ | 0 | ½ | 0 | ½ | 1 | * | 2½ | 2576 |

# OPENING ENCYCLOPAEDIA 2019

## NEW LAYOUT, BETTER ACCESS, EXCITING VIDEOS

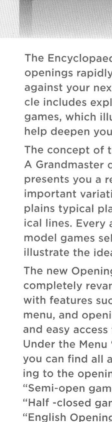

The Encyclopaedia can help you learn openings rapidly giving you a head start against your next opponents. Each article includes explanations and annotated games, which illustrate typical plans, to help deepen your understanding.

The concept of the opening article: A Grandmaster or International Master presents you a repertoire idea, shows all important variations and his analyses, explains typical plans and shows all the critical lines. Every article includes annotated model games selected by the author to illustrate the ideas in tournament practice.

The new Opening Encyclopaedia 2019 was completely revamped to enhance usability, with features such as a new design, new menu, and opening name sorting for fast and easy access to your favorite openings. Under the Menu "Ideas for your Repertoire" you can find all articles classified according to the opening names: "Open games", "Semi-open games", "Closed games", "Half -closed game", "Flank-Openings" or "English Opening and Reti". E.g. for the popular Najdorf Variation the Opening Encyclopaedia offers 41 opening articles. Each of it is accessible easily via "Semi-open games"- Siclian Defence – Najdorf Variation. As easy the user can switch from one article to the other to absorb all the important maneuvers and typical plans related to the variation. That way finding your favorite openings becomes easy and fast! Additionally, the new Encyclopaedia offers the traditional access to find openings from the "ECO-list" as an alternative access to all opening articles.

Also new: 20 high-class opening videos are included in the Encyclopaedia 2019, from our popular ChessBase Authors. You'll find Daniel King, Simon Williams, Yannick Pelletier, Mihail Marin, Erwin l'Ami, presenting new opening ideas clear and vividly. The number of articles in the Opening Encyclopaedia is growing – it now contains more than 1,100 and the included games database contains all games from all the opening articles. This makes the new Opening Encyclopaedia 2019 an indispensable reference for every tournament player.

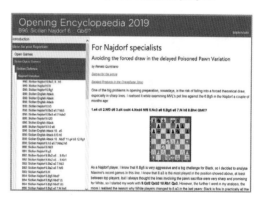

**All innovations at a glance:**

- Over 1,100 special theoretical databases
- 180 new opening surveys, a lot of them revised, in total 6,680 surveys
- Over 38,000 illustrative games
- Much improved usability: New design, new menu, new sorting of openings according to names for a fast and comfortable access
- 20 opening videos (total duration: 7 hours) of the most popular ChessBase Authors

Opening Encyclopaedia 2019    99,90 €

Update from
Opening Encyclopaedia 2018    59,90 €

ChessBase GmbH · News: en.chessbase.com · CB Shop: shop.chessbase.com
**CHESSBASE DEALER: NEW IN CHESS · P.O. Box 1093 · NL-1810 KB Alkmaar**
phone (+31)72 5127137 · fax (+31)72 5158234 · WWW.NEWINCHESS.COM

Judit Polgar

# When it's your move and you wish it weren't

Or, in perfect English: zugzwang! **JUDIT POLGAR** shows the charms of zugzwang, that wondrous phenomenon that decides many endgames. Highly frustrating when you're its victim; highly pleasing if you're on the right side of the board.

**Z**ugzwang has been one of my favourite themes since early childhood, even though I managed to use it only rarely in my own games. I would compare the slightly paradoxical situation of zugzwang with that of a soldier who has just stepped on a mine. Once he steps on the mine, it is not this action that kills him, but the necessity to keep moving. After he makes another step, no matter in which direction, the mine will explode.

It is hard to imagine the game of chess without zugzwang. The assessment of many endgames would be quite different if a player was not forced to make a move but had the choice to pass. Zugzwang allowed me to reach a clear draw in an unpleasant endgame against Alexei Shirov, in Dortmund in 1996, that I showed in an earlier column about endgame studies (see New In Chess 2018/6). In that case, zugzwang helped the defender, but more typically the active side makes use of it.

Here is an interesting example of White creating a far from obvious zugzwang situation.

**Fabiano Caruana**
**Parimarjan Negi**
Tromsø Olympiad 2014

position after 41...♚c7

White's advantage is beyond any doubt, but the question remains whether he will be able to make progress. His main ideas are taking control of the b-file and/or attacking the g7-pawn. But neither of these is achievable by a straightforward approach. What helps White is that all black pieces are placed optimally. The bishop is defended and covers the d-file, the rook controls the eighth rank (f8 in particular) and the b-file, and the king does not obstruct its action in any direction.

All these induce the thought that if White manages to pass the move to his opponent, Black will have to worsen his position himself.

**42.♖e1!?**

It's hard to say why Caruana preferred this over 42.♖d2, which would have eliminated all bishop moves due to ♖d7+. If, for instance, 42...♖a8 then 43.♖b2, with similar play as in the line from the next comment.

**'I witnessed this game with the feeling that it was one of the most remarkable clashes in this entire titanic battle.'**

**42...⌒d8**

This makes things simpler, leaving the most beautiful lines behind the scenes.

Unlike in the previous line, White had to count with the only possible bishop move, 42...♗g2. But now the bishop is no longer defended, allowing White to gain a decisive tempo in the following variation: 43.♖b1! (threatening 44.♗d6+!) 43...♔c8 (abandoning the b-file allows White a systematic win: 43...♖a8 44.♗c5 ♗d5 45.a3 ♖e8 46.♗b4 ♖a8 47.♔f4,

**ANALYSIS DIAGRAM**

and now zugzwang forces Black to give up the c4-pawn, when, after c3-c4, the rook will intrude via the d-file) 44.♖g1! (unpinning his own bishop with tempo) 44...♗d5 45.♗f8, with similar play as in the game.

**43.♗f8 ♖b7 44.e7+ ♔e8 45.♖e2!? ♖b1 46.♗xg7**

White took on h6 next and later won (1-0, 57).

Although zugzwang is usually associated with the endgame, there are exceptional circumstances in which it can occur in positions with many pieces on the board. Here is the most famous classical example:

**Alexander Alekhine**
**Aron Nimzowitsch**
San Remo 1930

position after 29...♔d8

**30.h4!**

Black will soon run out of pawn moves, and 30...♔e8 or 30...♕e8 will leave the c7-rook insufficiently defended, allowing b4-b5, winning a piece.

And here is a recent example of middlegame zugzwang:

**Viktor Bologan**
**Radoslaw Wojtaszek**
Reykjavik 2015

position after 28...♘f6

Bologan played: **29.♖f1,** retaining just an advantage.
He confessed that he had calculated the winning 29.♕g6! ♖c7 30.♖g1

♖h7 31.♖g2 without realizing Black had no useful moves left.

The rooks have to defend against ♕g8 and ♕g7 mate, advancing the pawns would clear the path for the b1-bishop, and any rook move along the seventh rank would release the pressure on h2, allowing the decisive ♖g5.

Sometimes, anticipating the possibility of zugzwang falls beyond the players' range even at the highest level. Here is an example from the latest world title match. I witnessed this game as a live commentator, with the feeling that it was one of the most remarkable clashes in this entire titanic battle.

**Magnus Carlsen**
**Fabiano Caruana**
London 2018 (6th match game)

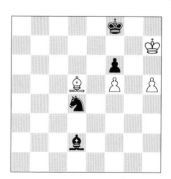

position after 66...♘d4

The World Champion had passed

through difficult moments earlier on, but then found the saving idea of moving his king to h7 on move 61. I believe that, starting from that moment, Caruana gave all credit to his opponent for his tenacity to fight for the draw and this may explain why he missed an 'unhuman' winning chance soon after.

Intuitively, we can feel that despite being material up, Black's win is at least problematic. In order to avoid immediate trouble, White needs to keep a few things in mind. He must not:

1) allow the enemy king to reach h8;

2) advance his h-pawn unless this leads to an obvious draw.

At the same time, he should find the optimal job distribution between his king and bishop, meaning that one of them needs to control g8 and the other has to defend f5. In many positions ...♘e2, threatening to go to either g3 or f4, would be decisive.

**67.♔g6?**

Carlsen decides to let the bishop control g8, noticing the threat (in the diagrammed position) 67...♘xf5 and if 68.♔g6 then 68...♘e7+, winning the bishop. For reasons explained in the next comment, this gives rise to the danger of zugzwang.

The correct job distribution was 67.♗c4!, controlling e2 with the bishop, which will later go to d3 to defend f5, and leaving the king with the task of controlling g8. When describing this move, I would once again use the term 'unhuman', due to its endless complexity, as the following analysis shows.

**ANALYSIS DIAGRAM**

67...♘xf5 leads to an amazing variation, at the end of which White reaches a positional draw: 68.♔g6 ♘d6. This gains a tempo for saving the f-pawn, but Black's imperfect coordination will prevent him from making progress: 69.♗e6 ♔e7 70.♗d5 f5 71.h6 ♗c3 72.h7 ♗d4 73.♔g5 ♗c3 74.♔g6.

**ANALYSIS DIAGRAM**

Amazingly, White's activity prevents Black from making progress. The only active attempt is 74...f4, but this exposes Black's last remaining pawn: 75.♔g5 ♗e5 76.h8♕, with a draw.

Or 67...♗g5 68.♗d3 ♗h4. This is the same kind of attempt at zugzwang as below, since the white bishop is tied to the defence of f5 and e2, but White has the reserve tempo 69.♔h8, and draws.

**67...♗g5 68.♗c4**

Caruana played **68...♘f3** and after **69.♔h7!** things took their normal course again and the game ended in a draw.

But Black had a fantastic resource with:

**68...♗h4!!**

Creating the first zugzwang. White loses control of e2.

For people watching the game with an engine, it was a shock to find out that

after White's last move there would be a mate in 36! To me, this did not come as a surprise, because I was already shocked that with correct play White should hold a draw!

**69.♗d5**

The best try, keeping the bishop active in the fight against the enemy knight. 69.h6 does not work due to 69...♘c6 70.h7 ♘e5+ 71.♔h5 (71.♔h6 is simpler: 71...♗g5+ 72.♔h5 ♔g7, and Black wins) 71...♔g7! 72.♔xh4 ♘xc4. In this line, the hanging c4-bishop was an additional element to the global piece relation.

**69...♘e2 70.♗f3**

Another beautiful line based on zugzwang is 70.♔h7 ♗g5 71.♗f3 ♘g3 72.♗g4 ♔f7 73.♔h8 (in order to make things simpler, the bishop should now reach f8, with the white king on h7) 73...♗c1 74.♔h7 ♗a3 (White is now forced to spoil his coordination) 75.♔h8 (if 75.h6 ♗f8 White cannot keep his f-pawn and prevent ...♘e4-g5+ at the same time) 75...♗f8 76.♔h7 ♘e4, followed by ...♘g5 and ...♗g7 and a quick mate.

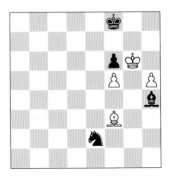

**70...♘g1!**

A paradoxical move, inviting White to

dominate the knight. It is an essential step on the way to zugzwang, with the aim of reaching h8 with the king.

**71.♗g4**

The thematic answer, because if White goes 71.♗d5, then after 71...♗g5 72.♔h7 ♘e2 73.♗f3 ♘g3 play will transpose to the line above.

**71...♔g8 72.♔h6**

The black king is optimally placed to restrict its rival and the knight is immobilised. But the white bishop is also stuck on g4, as it has to watch the knight, while the king has only g6 and h6 at its disposal. Black has a systematic way of passing the move to his opponent.

**72...♗e1**

72...♗g5+ 73.♔g6 reaches the critical position below, but with Black to move.

**73.♔g6 ♗c3 74.♔h6 ♗d2+ 75.♔g6 ♗g5**

Sadly for White, it is his move now.

**76.h6**

This is a concession already.

**76...♗h4**

The same thematic manoeuvre. The only difference now is that the white king has h5 and g6 at its disposal. 76...♗h8 also wins, but after 77.h7 Black would need to resort to the same method again, starting with 77...♗h4.

**77.♔h5 ♗e1 78.♔g6 ♗c3 79.♔h5 ♗d2 80.♔g6 ♗g5**

White soon loses the h-pawn and the game.

This game gave me a measure of the depths reached by our game. Without engines, would we have found Caruana's missed win?

## Conclusion

■ Zugzwang tends to occur in positions where one of the players is very passive.

■ Being aware of this, the defending side should strive for counterplay or at least some activity. ■

# A rook pawn march versus the Alekhine

**Jeroen Bosch**

**4. a4!?**

**Black has to solve lots of novel problems and will find it difficult to rely on his standard knowledge of the Alekhine.**

The Alekhine Defence is not among the most reliable responses to 1.e4, while paradoxically it was played by World Champions. Apart from the eponymous fourth World Champion, the names of Euwe, Fischer and Carlsen immediately spring to mind. Now it is my firm conviction that White can count on an opening advantage by playing the so-called Modern Variation (4.♘f3). So why do we need a surprise weapon?

Most White players encounter the Alekhine only rarely. The seasoned practitioners of the provocative knight move, on the other hand, will be able to practise their weapon in roughly half of their Black games, say one in every four games that they play. Clearly they will have an edge in knowledge and understanding from the moment 1.e4 ♘f6 appears on the board. If we take this into account, then a small surprise on our part won't hurt, right?

**1.e4 ♘f6 2.e5 ♘d5 3.c4**

This is the move order we will use to introduce our weapon. It's useful to know, though, that many of the positions that we will investigate below may arise from the regular move order of the Exchange Variation: 3.d4 d6 4.c4 ♘b6 5.exd6, and now, after 5...cxd6 6.♘c3 g6, White only infrequently launches his rook pawn, but 7.a4!? ♗g7 (7...a5 8.c5 see below)

8.a5 ♘6d7 is one of the main positions of our SOS. Likewise, after 5...exd6 White can also play 6.a4!?, when 6...a5! transposes to one of our main lines.

**3...♘b6 4.a4!?**

And this is it! There is no rest for the weary! The knight that has already moved thrice is to be further persecuted by this march of the rook pawn. Black now has to make up his mind: he may either stop the a-pawn in its tracks with 4...a5, or he may decide to ignore this flank move by countering in the centre with his programmed 4...d6 (or even 4...d5).

Variation A – 4...d6
Variation B – 4...a5

## Variation A
**4...d6**

The regular Alekhine move is 4...d6, to immediately attack the advanced e-pawn. White then continues with what he has been doing so far, which is gain tempi and space.

After 4...d5?!, 5.exd6 would simply transpose to 4...d6 5.a5 ♘6d7 6.exd6 below, with admittedly the added advantage for Black that he has prevented the 6.e6 option (which I would not recommend for White anyway).

However, White is well-advised to accept the challenge and play 5.c5 when 5...♘c4 6.d4 gives White a huge space advantage, and the intrepid

Alekhine knight on c4 is in all likelihood a liability rather than a source for counterplay.

**5.a5 ♘6d7**

**6.exd6**

In practice, White often goes for the sharp 6.e6!?, when play continues 6...fxe6 7.d4. Best for Black now is the immediate 7...e5! 8.♗d3 g6, when Black is doing well after 9.h4 (Snigurov-Bortnyk, Lutsk 2018)

and now 9...exd4! 10.h5 ♘c5 11.hxg6 h6, when Black's central preponderance is more important than White's attacking chances. If White instead goes 9.d5, Black should play 9...♗g7 or 9...♘c5.

After 6.exd6 Black has to make up his mind about taking back on d6.

Variation A1 – 6...exd6
Variation A2 – 6...cxd6

## Variation A1

After the symmetrical **6...exd6** White goes **7.d4 ♗e7 8.♘f3** Klimchuk-Vovk, Kiev 2017, went 8.♗d3 ♘f6?! 9.♘e2 ♘c6 10.♗e3 ♘b4 11.0-0 ♘xd3 12.♕xd3 0-0 13.♘bc3, which gave White some edge, but

Black need not limit his choices with 8...♗f6.

**8...0-0 9.♗d3** when he can be happy with his space advantage.

For example:
– 9...♘c6 10.0-0 (more accurate is 10.♘c3!, in order to meet 10...♘b4 with 11.♗b1) 10...♘b4 11.♗e2 ♘f6 (11...♘b8!?) 12.♗d2 d5 13.c5 ♘c6 (Riabko-Panchenko, Kiev 2010), and now 14.♘c3, followed by ♗f4, is slightly better for White.
– 9...♖e8 10.0-0 ♘c6 (Dolezal-Alvarez, Villa Martelli 2004), and now White should simply continue his development with 11.♘c3, when he has a favourable version of the regular ...exd6 Exchange Variation: Black has lost some time and the pawn on a5 is quite annoying for Black. On move 10 Black may consider 10...c5 or 10...♘f6.

## Variation A2

**6...cxd6 7.d4 g6** It's normal to fianchetto the king's bishop in the Exchange Variation with ...cxd6. Worse is 7...e6 8.♘f3 ♗e7 9.♗e2 ♘f6 10.♘c3 0-0 11.0-0 d5. We have a completely normal position here in which Black has lost about three tempi.

**8.♘f3 ♗g7**

Here White has several decent options:

■ It is amusing to start with **9.♖a3 0-0 10.♗e2** 10.♘c3! is best and transposes to 9.♘c3 0-0 10.♖a3. **10...e5** 10...d5 11.0-0 dxc4 12.♘bd2 b5 13.axb6 ♘xb6 is equal, Ponkratov-Volodin, Izhevsk 2011. **11.dxe5** 11.0-0!. **11...dxe5** 11...♘xe5 12.0-0 ♘bc6, with counterplay. **12.♘c3 ♘c6** was equal in Firman-Bernadskiy, Golden Sands 2015.

■ The line **9.♘c3 0-0 10.♖a3!?** has been played in more than two dozen games (the stem game was Alexandria-Gipslis from 1977). After **10...♘c6** we see the point of the rook move. **11.d5!**

when 11...♘xa5? loses to 12.b4. White has an edge after 11...♘ce5 12.♘d4. So, best for Black is **11...♘b4** but even here White has several decent ways towards an opening plus.

■ A very decent pawn sac is **9.♗e2 0-0 10.0-0 ♘c6 11.d5! ♘xa5 12.♗d2** Worthy of attention is 12.♖a2!?, Schulze-Biehler, Germany 1989, intending 12...b6 13.b4 ♘b7 14.♘d4, and White has ample compensation for the pawn. **12...b6 13.♗c3**

**13...♘e5** 13...♘f6 14.b4 ♘b7 15.♘d4 a5 16.♘c6 ♕e8 (16...♕c7) 17.♗f3 (17.♕d4!) 17...e5?! 18.dxe6 fxe6, Bortnyk-Terentjev, Kemer 2009, and here 19.♕d4! would have given White a substantial edge. **14.♘d4 ♗d7** 14...♘axc4 15.♗xc4 ♘xc4 16.♘c6 ♕d7 17.♗xg7 ♔xg7 18.♕d4+ ♘e5 19.f4 f6 is not entirely clear, but in any case better for White. **15.b3 g5** The threat was f4. **16.♘d2 ♘b7 17.♘2f3 h6 18.♘xe5 ♗xe5**

and in this position White is better (Black's extra pawn hardly counts) after normal moves like 19.♗d3 or 19.♕c2, as long as he does not try to force matters with 19.♘c6? ♗xc6 20.dxc6 ♘a5 – Firman-Neverov, Ordzhonikidze 2001.

## Variation B
**4...a5**

Black stops the march of the a-pawn. The pawn on a5 may either have weakened the queenside (square b6 becomes more vulnerable), or it may in fact have strengthened Black's play here (square b4 may become an outpost for a knight).
**5.d4**

The fun-move is of course 5.♖a3?!, and this has indeed occurred quite a few times in practice. 5...d6 6.exd6 exd6 7.♖g3 (7.d4 transposes to a position I will mention below) 7...♗f5 is a suggestion of Cox's (in his book *Starting Out: Alekhine Defence,* 2004) in reply to 5.♖a3 (a move he never saw played). Fairly recently this has been tried out in practice: 8.♘c3 ♘c6 9.d4 ♘b4 10.♗e2. Black should be better here, but his next move squanders his edge: 10...d5?! 11.c5 ♘d7 12.♗g4 ♕e7+ 13.♘ge2 ♗xg4 14.♖xg4 ♘f6 15.♖g3 ♕d7 16.♗f4 ♗e7 17.♗e5 0-0 18.♕d2 ♔h8

19.♖xg7?! (White is a bit better here and objectively has no reason to force a draw. However, Black is a strong GM, which explains Hauge's decision) 19...♔xg7 20.♕g5+ ♔h8 21.♗xf6+ ♗xf6 22.♕xf6+ ♔g8 23.♕g5+ ½-½, Hauge-Agdestein, Stavanger 2017.
Of course Black can take with the c-pawn as well on move 6: after 6...cxd6 7.d4 (7.♖g3 is the most popular move – chess players have a sense of humour too!) 7...g6 (7...♘c6) 8.♘f3 ♗g7 9.♗e2 0-0 10.0-0 is untested and about equal.
**5...d6 6.exd6** After the text we have the same division as above, since Black may take back with either the e- or the c-pawn.

Variation B1 – 6...cxd6
Variation B2 – 6...exd6

## Variation B1
**6...cxd6 7.♘c3 g6**
The interpolation of 4.a4 a5 appears

to favour White here. He now usually plays the sharp:
**8.c5! dxc5 9.♗b5+ ♘6d7**
The only move. 9...♗d7? 10.dxc5 ♘c8 11.♕d4; 9...♘c6? 10.d5; 9...♘8d7? 10.dxc5.
**10.♗f4 ♗g7 11.♘d5**

There are some 50 games in the database with this position! Most of them arose via the traditional move order in the Exchange Variation. Here we need to delve a little deeper.

## Variation B11
Let's first note that **11...0-0?!** loses an exchange: **12.♗c7 ♕e8 13.♘b6 ♖a6**

and now not 14.♘xd7? ♗xd7 15.♗xa6 ♘xa6 16.♗e5, Riff-Ehlvest, Berlin 2015, but **14.dxc5 ♘c6 15.♗xa6 bxa6 16.♘e2** with a clear edge in Somlai-Varhegyi, Hungary blitz 1990.

## Variation B12
Interesting is **11...e5!? 12.dxe5**
Or 12.♗xe5!? 0-0 13.♗xg7 (Black has counterplay after 13.♗c7 ♕g5) 13...♔xg7 14.dxc5 ♘c6 15.♘e2, and now Black should play 15...♘xc5

(rather than 15...♘ce5? 16.♖c1, with an extra pawn, in Janev-Gozzoli, Cannes 2002) 16.0-0 ♗f5, when he has nearly equalized.

**12...0-0 13.♘f3 ♘b6!**

13...♘c6 14.♗g5 (14.♗xc6 bxc6 15.♗g5) 14...f6 15.♘xf6+ ♗xf6 16.♕b3+ ♔h8 17.0-0 ♘d4 18.♗xd4 cxd4 favours White.

**14.♘f6+ ♗xf6 15.exf6 ♕xf6 16.♗e5 ♕e6** 16...♕f5! **17.0-0 ♘c6 18.♖e1** 18.♗g3±. **18...♘xe5 19.♖xe5 ♕f6 20.♖xc5 ♕xb2** and Black was slightly better in Jäckle-Schnabel, Germany 1992.

### Variation B13
**11...♘a6**

This is an important position.

Let's first note that 12.dxc5? 0-0 13.♖c1 e6! 14.♘c3 e5 15.♗e3 ♘dxc5 is no good; Salmensuu-Solozhenkin, Finland 2000.

Instead, 12.♕e2 has been successfully tried in practice, but nobody has replied with the sharp 12...0-0, when 13.♘xe7+ ♔h8 14.d5 ♘c7 15.♘f3 ♘xb5 16.axb5 ♘f6 gives Black plenty of play as well.

Let's now delve into the complications with **12.♗xa6**, which is met by **12...e5! 13.♗b5**

13.♗g5? ♕xg5 14.♘c7+ ♔f8 15.♘xa8 ♕xg2 16.♕f3 ♕xf3 17.♘xf3 bxa6 and Black wins; 13.♗xe5? ♘xe5; 13.dxe5 ♖xa6 14.♘f3 ♖e6!.

**13...exf4 14.♕e2+ ♔f8 15.♘f3 ♘f6**

Here 15...cxd4 16.0-0 ♘f6 17.♘xf4 ♕d6 is given as equal by Cox. And 15...♗xd4 is probably good enough for equality as well: 16.♘xd4 cxd4

17.0-0 ♕g5 (17...♔g7!=) 18.♘c7 ♘e5, Ansell-Cox, London League 2004, and now 19.♕e4! ♖b8 20.h4! ♕e7 21.♘d5 is still better for White.

**16.♘xf4 cxd4 17.0-0 ♗f5 18.♖fe1 ♕d6** was equal in Savory-Carleton, Liverpool 2006.

Now let's go back to the position after 11...♘a6. I would like to recommend the untested 12.♗g5!? f6 13.♗e3 as an improvement for White.

### Variation B2
**6...exd6** With the interpolation of a4 a5 this makes a lot of sense. Square b4 is a rather tasty pasture for a Black knight.

**7.♘c3** In case of 7.♗d3 ♘c6 8.♗e3, Timothy Taylor indicates 8...♘b4 with equality in his *Alekhine Alert!* (2010). Here, 8...g6 looks fine too by the way.

A young Anna Muzychuk twice played 7.♖a3!?, but Black is objectively fine after 7...♘c6 8.♘g3 ♗f5, A.Muzychuk-Petrenko, Istanbul 2003.

**7...♘c6** Practice has also seen 7...♗e7 8.♘f3 0-0 9.♗e2 ♗g4 10.0-0 ♘c6 11.b3 ♗f6 12.♗e3, and objectively the chances should be equal.

Two examples:

– 12...♘e7?! (the wrong knight goes to e7) 13.h3 ♗xf3 14.♗xf3 d5 15.c5 ♘bc8 16.♕d3±; Degtiarev-Will, Reykjavik 2011.

– 12...d5 13.c5 ♘c8 14.h3 ♗xf3 15.♗xf3 ♘8e7! 16.g4 g6 (16...h6!?) 17.♔g2, with approximately equal chances in M.Muzychuk-Zhukova, Moscow blitz 2010.

**8.♗e3 d5** A sharp attempt; Black can also continue his development with 8...♗f5 or 8...♗e7.

**9.c5** White must accept the challenge. **9...♘c4 10.♗xc4 dxc4 11.♕e2 ♘b4** This was Black's idea behind 8...d5: White has no useful discovered check, while Black is threatening ...♘d3+ and ...♗f5.

**12.0-0-0** Correct was 12.♖d1!. The game is pretty sharp, with chances for both sides. In case of 12...♘d3+?!, 13.♔f1 ♗f5 14.b3 leaves White somewhat better.

**12...♘d3+** Or simply 12...♗e7. **13.♖xd3?!** After 13.♔b1 ♗e7 14.b3 0-0 15.bxc4 ♘b4 Black has ample compensation for the pawn. The White king is rather too 'airy' on the queenside.

**13...cxd3 14.♕xd3 ♗e7 15.♘f3 0-0 16.d5 ♗f6** and White had insufficient compensation for the exchange in Mazarov-Jugelt, Dortmund 2006.

In the final analysis, 4.a4 may not be enough to promise an edge, but we have seen that there are many pitfalls for Black. The second player has to solve lots of novel problems and will find it difficult to rely on his standard knowledge of the Alekhine. ■

## The Blitz Whisperer
### Maxim Dlugy

# Generation Gap

Are the new rising grandmasters really as good as their ratings suggest? Certainly not in all aspects of the game, **MAXIM DLUGY** contends. Taking a closer look at the blitz games he himself played against the young superstars, he detects weaknesses and shows what they still have to work on.

**A**t the International Children and Youth Festival in Vilnius in the last week of March, co-organized by the Kasparov Foundation, Garry Kasparov gave an interesting interview to Evgeny Surov of the website chess-news. The former World Champion subtly pointed to the possibility that today's young superstar grandmasters are perhaps not as strong as their titles and ratings suggest. He referred to Bobby Fischer's qualification to the Candidates tournament at age 15, and at his own joint first place in the USSR Championship at age 18.

One may wonder, is it chess rating inflation or the way kids study chess in the computer-driven age that separates these generations? As I continue to play online blitz against these young talents, I sometimes also wonder if there is something missing in the new generation that allows us 50+ guys to still give them a match – provided we've had a good night's rest?

Let me showcase some of my games against today's young stars to try and explain what may be missing in these youngsters' games and what they can work on to improve their play.

### Sharp from the start

When playing blitz online, it usually takes me a game or two to get rolling, but with Alireza Firouzja, the 15-year-old sensation from Iran (he won the national championship when he was 12!), I never get the chance, because he usually flags me from a bad position in the first game we play, and then refuses to give me a rematch. In the following game I decided to concentrate fully on Game One to avoid this unpleasantness.

**MaximDlugy**
**Firouzja2003**
Chess.com Live Chess 2019
Pirc Defence

**1.d4 ♘f6 2.♗f4 g6 3.♘c3** This has been my favourite setup against the King's Indian and Grünfeld complex for the last few years.
**3...♗g7 4.e4 d6 5.♕d2 0-0 6.0-0-0**

**6...♘c6** The most common move played by top-grandmasters against me. The problem is that 6...♘bd7 is strongly met by 7.e5!.
**7.f3**

**7...a6** The thematic 7...e5 is no good, since White gets a free pawn or more in the variation 8.dxe5 dxe5 9.♕xd8 ♖xd8 10.♖xd8+ ♘xd8 11.♗xe5 ♘xe4 12.♗xg7 ♘f2 13.♗d4 ♘xh1 14.g4 ♘c6 15.♗e3 h5 16.♗g2 hxg4 17.♗xh1.
**8.♗h6** White's strategy is to weaken the kingside and play against the black king. There is no reason why

Black should not be slightly worse in this set-up.

**8...e5 9.♗xg7 ♔xg7 10.♘ge2 b5 11.h4** Starting the attack. As you will see from the next game against Vladimir Fedoseev, 11.g4! may be an even stronger option.

**11...h5 12.dxe5 dxe5**

It seems safer to take with the knight, although after 12...♘xe5 13.♘f4 ♖b8 14.♔b1 ♗b7 15.♗e2, I still prefer White's chances.

**13.♕g5!**

The queen is very strong here and Black will have to be alert to tactical ideas.

**13...♕e7 14.♘g3**

Now I am threatening both 15.♘f5+ and 15.♘d5, with an advantage.

**14...♘d4??**

A blunder, although Black is much worse already.

Instead, after 14...♔h7 15.♘d5 ♘xd5 16.exd5 ♕xg5+ 17.hxg5 ♘e7 18.c4!, White defends the d5-pawn and prepares ♖e1, with a large advantage.

**15.♘xh5+**

Winning everything.

In this game, the young Iranian grandmaster showed that he is not

fully familiar with the ideas of the system, although White's plan, made famous by Bobby Fischer's onslaughts in the Yugoslav Attack against the Dragon, should have rung a bell.

About 10 minutes after I finished the previous game, Vladimir Fedoseev,

**Alireza Firouzja: not familiar with Bobby Fischer's onslaughts against the Dragon?**

the 24-year-old St Petersburg grandmaster, accepted my challenge and went right into the same line as the Iranian GM.

**MaximDlugy
Bigfish1995 (=Fedoseev)**
Chess.com Live Chess 2019
Pirc Defence

**1.d4 ♘f6 2.♗f4 g6 3.♘c3 ♗g7 4.e4 d6 5.♕d2 0-0 6.0-0-0 ♘c6 7.f3 a6 8.♗h6 e5 9.♗xg7 ♔xg7 10.♘ge2 b5**

This time, having briefly analysed my

previous game, I decided to thwart Black's ...h5 in an attempt to get an even larger advantage in the opening. **11.g4!?**

**11...h5**

Black tries to blunt my attack immediately with a typical King's Indian advance, but what works with the dark-squared bishops on the board, turns out to be strategically dubious here.

Perhaps a better plan for Black is to force White's play with 11...b4. Now, after 12.♘d5 ♘xd5 13.exd5 ♘xd4 14.♘xd4 exd4 15.♕xd4+ (after 15.g5!? a possible continuation could be 15...f6 16.h4! fxg5 17.hxg5 ♔g8 18.f4 ♗g4 19.♖e1 ♖e8 20.♕xb4 ♗f3 21.♗h3!? ♗xh1 – he should take on d5 with the bishop – 22.♖xe8+ ♕xe8 23.♗e6+ ♔f8 24.♕xd4, and White wins) Black equalizes with 15...♕f6 16.♕xb4 ♕xf3 17.♕d4+ ♔g8 18.♖g1 ♖e8 19.♗d3 ♕e3+ 20.♕xe3 ♖xe3. So White should experiment with 15.g5!?, delaying the recapture of the d4-pawn to keep control of the queen.
**12.h3!?**

This simple move delays the opening of the files on the kingside and ties Black's knight to the defence of the h5-pawn. I could also have played 12.dxe5, but I didn't want to create a crisis on the board so soon.

**12...♖h8 13.♗g2**

## 'In the first game we play, Firouzja usually flags me from a bad position and then refuses to give me a rematch.'

I connect rooks and prepare the f4-break. Black must act quickly now or I will play g5, followed by dxe5 and f4.

**13...b4 14.♘d5 ♘xd5 15.exd5 ♘xd4 16.♘xd4 exd4 17.♕xd4+ ♕f6**

This version of the position, where my bishop is on g2, protecting the f3-pawn, is clearly in my favour. Black will need to find compensation for the b-pawn.

**18.♕xb4 ♗d7 19.♕d4 ♖ab8**

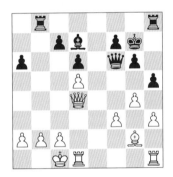

**20.g5?!**

An inaccuracy. I wanted to fix Black's pawns on light squares, but there was no need to, as they weren't running anywhere.

It was more important to quickly activate the rook with 20.♕xf6+ ♔xf6 21.♖d4!. Now I would tie Black down to the defence of the c7-pawn, with a sizable advantage.

**20...♕xd4 21.♖xd4 ♖he8 22.b3**

Another inaccuracy, allowing Black to fully equalize.

After 22.h4 a5 23.b3 ♖e2 24.♗h3 ♗xh3 25.♖xh3 ♖b4! Black's activity would be sufficient to hold the game, but the ...a5/...♖b4 plan is not so easy to find.

**22...f6?** Vladimir should have activated his rook. After 22...♖e2 23.♖d2

Vladimir Fedoseev missed a few equalizing lines in the endgame.

♖be8 24.h4 a5 25.♖hd1 f6!, followed by ...♗f5, White has no way to improve his position.

**23.f4 fxg5 24.fxg5 ♗f5**

**25.h4?** My turn to be inaccurate. I should have tied Black down to the c7-pawn immediately with 25.♖c4!, with a large advantage.

**25...♖e2 26.♖d2 ♖be8 27.♗f1?**

And this is simply wrong, as I had missed Black's 30th move. After 27.♖hd1!, threatening to trade off rooks, followed by ♖d2, I would maintain an advantage.

**27...♖e1+ 28.♖d1 ♗g4! 29.♖xe1 ♖xe1+ 30.♔d2**

**30...♖a1?** Fedoseev misses the key defensive idea in the position – the intermediate check. After 30...♖d1+ 31.♔e3 ♖e1+ the king cannot venture too far from the queenside or from the bishop on f1, as Black always has ...♗f3 and ...♗e2, so a draw is secured.

**31.♗g2!** Black now restores material equality, but my pawn structure and active rook give me a nearly decisive advantage.

**31...♖xa2 32.♖e1 ♗f5 33.♗e4?**

Oops, the ♖e7xc7 manoeuvre would defend the c2-pawn.

Hand-playing had begun, as we were deep below the one-minute mark.

**33...♗d7?** Black's chance was in getting counterplay against the d5-pawn. After 33...♗xe4 34.♖xe4 ♖a5! 35.♖e7+ ♔f8 36.♖xc7 ♖xd5+ 37.♔e3 ♖d1 the attack on the h-pawn gives Black good survival chances.

**34.♗d3!**

Black cannot protect both the c7- and g6-targets without his rook.

**34...♔f7 35.♖f1+ ♔g7 36.♖f6 ♗e8 37.♖e6 ♗f7 38.♖e7 ♖a1 39.♖xc7 ♖h1**

**40.♗xa6?!** Natural in time-pressure but inaccurate. I should have concentrated on my own strengths, the c- and d-pawns.

After the straightforward 40.c4 ♖xh4 41.♖d7 ♖g4 42.♖xd6 h4 43.♖xa6 h3 44.♖a1 ♖xg5 45.♖h1 ♖h5 46.♔e3 g5 47.♗f5 h2 48.♔f3 ♔f6 49.♗g4 ♖h8 50.♔g3 ♖b8 51.♗d1 White wins.

**40...♖xh4 41.♗c8?!**

During the game I was fairly happy with this move, stopping the advance of the h-pawn while threatening ♗e6, but the immediate 41.c4 ♖h2+ 42.♔e1 h4 43.c5 h3 44.cxd6 ♖a2 45.♗e2 h2 46.♗f3, although quite unnatural, appears to be stronger.

**41...♔f8 42.♗e6?** A mistake. In an attempt to make the position simpler, I am giving Black real drawing chances. 42.c4 was still winning.

**42...♗e8?**

He believes me! After the correct 42...♗xe6 43.dxe6 ♖g4 44.c4 h4 45.♖h7 ♔e8 46.♔c3 ♖xg5 47.♖xh4 ♖g3+ 48.♔b2 ♔e7 49.♖e4 ♖g2+ 50.♔c3 g5 51.b4 g4 52.b5 g3 Black escapes with a draw.

**43.c4**

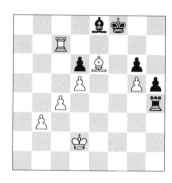

Now that I have finally played c4, it's all over.

**43...♖h2+ 44.♔c3 ♖g2 45.b4 ♖g3+ 46.♔d4 ♖xg5 47.b5 ♖g1 48.b6 ♖b1 49.b7 h4 50.♖h7 g5 51.c5 ♖b4+ 52.♔c3 dxc5 53.d6 g4 54.♖h8+ ♔g7 55.♖xe8 ♖xb7 56.♖e7+ ♔f6 57.♖xb7 ♔xe6 58.♖h7 h3 59.d7** 1-0.

In this game, Fedoseev did not fully equalize in the opening, but, more importantly, missed a number of equalizing lines in the endgame.

## 35-year age difference

The young Iranian grandmaster Parham Maghsoodloo was the World Junior Champion last year, having won the event with 9½/11, a point ahead of his competitors. I also won this championship a point ahead of my nearest rivals, in 1985, and one would assume that the 35-year difference in our ages should tilt the scales in the youngster's favour. Yet, though at the time of writing Parham is number 2 on chess.com's roster, behind Hikaru Nakamura, my score against him is positive. On an otherwise uneventful February afternoon, I even managed to beat him five times in a row. Let's have a look at one of his games, looking for generation gap weaknesses.

**Parhamov (= Maghsoodloo)**
**MaximDlugy**
Chess.com Live Chess 2017
Réti, King's Indian Attack

**1.♘f3 ♘f6 2.g3 g6 3.♗g2 ♗g7 4.0-0 0-0 5.d3**

The new school of chess, recently supported by Magnus Carlsen, has many young talents thinking that opening preparation is not as important as good middlegame strategy. This begs the question: how to learn good middlegame strategy if you haven't analysed a slew of opening positions and the related plans?

**5...d5 6.♘bd2 c5 7.e4 ♘c6 8.♖e1 e5** Of course, there is nothing wrong with playing the King's Indian as White, that is, with an extra tempo, but clearly White is not vying for any kind of pressure or advantage in such cases.

**9.a4 d4**

The old books say: take space if it doesn't cost you anything.

**10.♘c4 ♕c7 11.c3 ♗e6**

White's strongest minor, the c4-knight, needs to be eliminated.

**12.cxd4 ♗xc4**

**13.dxc4?**

Surprisingly a mistake. Young talents should be trained to look for intermediate moves. After 13.dxe5! ♖fd8! 14.exf6 ♗xf6 15.e5 ♗e7 16.♗f4 ♕c8 17.♘g5 ♖xd3 18.♕c2 ♗a6 the position is balanced and full of life.

**13...cxd4** White's strategy has already backfired, and Mikhail Botvinnik would have pronounced White strategically lost here.

**14.♗d2 a5 15.h4 ♘d7** Now I just need to place the pieces on the correct spots.

**16.h5 ♘c5 17.b3 ♖fe8 18.♖b1 ♖a6!** I remember this manoeuvre from Fischer-Keres and Smyslov-Gligoric games. Now, with the pressure on the b3-pawn and the control of the 6th rank, my kingside will be safe, while White's b-pawn will tie him down badly.

**19.♕e2? ♘b6 20.♕d1 ♕d7 21.♘h2 ♘b4 22.♗g4**
This aggressive move is simply wrong, since there is nothing to be done about me capturing the h-pawn.

**22...gxh5! 23.♘h2 h4!**
This weakens the f4-square, which, after the exchange of dark-squared bishops, will cost White dearly.

**24.gxh4 ♘cd3 25.♖f1 ♗h6! 26.♔h1 ♗xd2 27.♕xd2 ♘f4 28.♖g1 ♔h8 29.♗f3 ♕h3**

My pieces are getting involved with White's king now.

**30.♖g4 ♖h6?**
An inaccuracy, giving White some

Parham Maghsoodloo: lack of understanding of the King's Indian pawn structure?

chances. 30...♘bd3 would leave no hope.

**31.♗g2?** White should have tried the sacrificial 31.♖xf4 exf4 32.h5!, although Black is still close to winning after 32...♖d6 33.♕xf4 ♕e6.

**31...♕d3 32.♕xd3 ♘bxd3 33.♖f1 ♖b6 34.♘f3 ♖xb3 35.♔h2 ♘xg2 36.♖xg2 ♘f4 37.♖g3**

As time is getting short, I decide to start hunting pawns.

**37...♖b4 38.♖fg1 ♘e2 39.♘xe5 ♘xg3 40.♘xf7+ ♔g7 41.♘d6 ♖d8 42.e5**

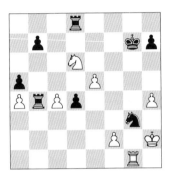

**42...♖b3!** After this White doesn't get the open file.

**43.fxg3 d3 44.♖d1 ♔f8 45.♔g2 ♔e7 46.♔f3 ♔e6 47.♔e4**

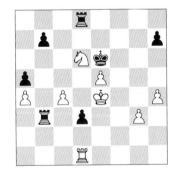

**47...♖g8!** Unfortunately for White, he has too many loose pawns that my rooks can cling to. Black is winning.

**48.♔f4 h5 49.♘e4 ♖g4+ 50.♔f3 d2+**

In this game White showed a lack of understanding of the King's Indian pawn structure, which allowed me to gradually use the extra space to target his weaknesses and win the game.

Although Pavel Eljanov is already 36 years old, he is still one generation behind me. So when I play him I still feel like I am playing in the more mature role. In the following game, the strategic plan Black opted for simply backfired.

**MaximDlugy**
**eljanov**
Chess.com Live Chess 2019
Queen's Indian, Classical Variation

1.d4 ♘f6 2.c4 e6 3.♘f3 b6 4.g3 ♗b7 5.♗g2 ♗e7 6.♘c3 ♘e4 7.♗d2 ♗f6 8.♕c2 ♘xd2 9.♕xd2 0-0 10.e4 d6 11.0-0 g6 12.♖fe1 ♗g7 13.♖ad1 ♘d7 14.h4

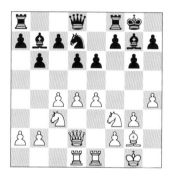

Back in 1985, when I played Viktor Kortchnoi in the Toronto International, we analysed this position for over two hours, with Viktor being unable to prove full equality. I still think White's centre and space are worth more than the two bishops. It's just that I need to find the moves to prove it.

**14...h6 15.b3 a6 16.d5**
At the end of the day, it's this move, shutting out the b7-bishop, that forces Black to make some tough decisions.

**16...♕e7 17.h5 g5 18.♘d4**

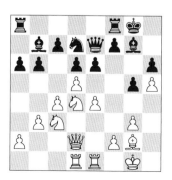

The engine thinks Black is fully OK if he keeps the pawn on e6. But in view of my plans (forcing the pawn to move with ♗h3) it makes it look as if Black – who then would need to play ...e5 – made a logical choice.

**18...♗xd4?!**
If Black is to play ...e5, he'd better trade the bishop first, as otherwise it will be buried. The problem is that

Pavel Eljanov saw his strategic plan backfire.

in this case White has a free space advantage on the queenside without the need to ward off two bishops.

**19.♕xd4 e5 20.♕d2 ♘f6**
Now Black starts playing against the h5-pawn. Will he be able to get it?

**21.♗f3 ♔h7 22.♔g2 g4 23.♗e2 ♖g8 24.♖h1 ♖g5 25.♖h4 ♖ag8 26.♖dh1**

It's clear that White will not be losing the h-pawn anytime soon. What does that mean? To me it means that White has a huge advantage on the queenside, which Black must attend to as soon as possible.

**26...♗c8 27.♗d3**
I am completing the regrouping of my pieces to optimal spots. The bishop will protect e4 and stop the ...f5 break, while the knight will double its efforts from e3.

**27...a5 28.♘d1 ♖8g7 29.♘e3 ♗d7** Everything is now ready for my attack on the queenside.

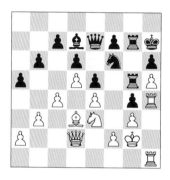

**30.a3 ♕d8?** The queen is a bad defender against the rooks that are coming to invade. Black should have sent the rook to the queenside, although White's advantage is quite significant even after 30...♖g8.

**31.♕c3 ♘g8 32.b4 axb4 33.axb4**

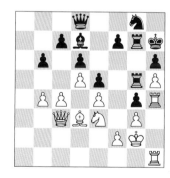

**33...♘f6?!**
Black's last chance was to find counterplay with 33...c5, though even after 34.♕a3, followed by ♕a7, Black would be in serious trouble.

**34.c5 bxc5 35.bxc5 ♕a8?**
The queen is in the wrong neighbourhood here.

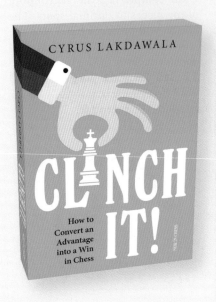
## 'This nagging feeling that somehow the endgame knowledge is not up to par in the younger generation continued to bug me.'

**36.c6 ♗c8 37.♖a1 ♕b8**

**38.♖hh1!**
Completing the puzzle. Both Black's queen and bishop are running out of moves.
**38...♕b6 39.♖hb1 ♕c5 40.♕xc5 dxc5 41.♖b8 ♖g8 42.♖aa8**
The bishop is trapped, so Pavel resigned.
In this game, an old strategic pattern was never countered by Black. Eljanov lost the game, not because he made any particular blunder, but because he believed in Black's pawn structure, which was by my standards untenable.

### Issues in simple endgames
Recently I was lucky enough to score 4 out of 5 when playing blitz online against Daniil Dubov, the reigning World Rapid Champion, who was clearly off form that day.

Still, this nagging feeling that somehow the endgame knowledge is not up to par in the younger generation continued to bug me, as game after game I keep seeing issues in more or less simple endgames that befall them.

In the following game against Dubov, I had Black and found myself in an unpleasant endgame after the 30th move.

**Duhless (= Dubov)**
**MaxADlugy**
Chess.com Live Chess 2019

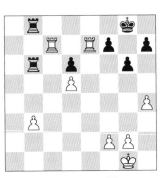

position after 30.♖exe7

Is it possible to win such a position with Black? Not against the World Rapid Champion, right?
**30...♖f8 31.♖b7 ♖xb7 32.♖xb7 ♖c8** I was hoping to draw by activating my rook.
**33.b4 ♖c4 34.g3 ♖d4 35.♖b5 ♔g7 36.♔g2 ♔f6 37.♔f3**

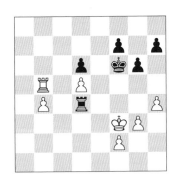

**37...♔e5?!** An inaccuracy. As White will try to pick off my pawns on the 7th rank, I should have started with ...h5. After 37...h5 38.♔e3 ♖d1 39.♔e4 ♖e1+ 40.♔d4 ♖d1+ 41.♔c4 ♖c1+ 42.♔b3 ♖b1+! White's king cannot escape the mad rook.
**38.♔e3 ♖d1** Oops, I realized just in time that I cannot go into the king and pawn ending by taking on d5. After 38...♖xd5 39.♖xd5+ ♔xd5

40.♔d3 Black runs out of moves
rather quickly.
**39.♖b7 ♔f6 40.♔e4 ♖b1 41.b5
♖b4+ 42.♔d3 h5**

**43.b6?**
This is inaccurate. White should
have brought the king in first. After
43.♔c3 ♖b1 44.♔c4 ♖c1+ 45.♔b4
♔e5 46.♖xf7 the win shouldn't be
too far.
**43...♔e5**

**44.♖xf7?**
The bait worked! White should
have kept his biggest trump – the
b-pawn. After 44.♔c3 ♖b1 45.♔c4
♔f6 46.♖b8 ♔e7 47.f3 ♔f6 48.♖b7
g5! 49.hxg5+ ♔xg5 50.♖b8 ♔f6
51.b7 ♔e7 52.g4 h4 53.g5 h3 54.g6
h2 55.♖h8 fxg6 56.♖xh2 ♔f6 Black
seems to hold by a hair's breadth.
**44...♖xb6 45.♔e2?**
Now the position is equal, because
White misses a simple check to
protect the pawn.
**45...♖b8 46.♖e7+ ♔xd5 47.♖g7
♖e8+ 48.♔f3 ♖e6 49.♔f4 ♔c4**
I need to activate the d-pawn for
counterplay.
**50.♖c7+ ♔d3 51.♖d7 ♔d4
52.♔g5 d5**

Daniil Dubov: work to do in the endgame?

**53.f4** Not the cleanest way to create
a passed pawn; f3/g4 would be much
simpler.
**53...♔e4 54.g4 hxg4 55.♔xg4
d4**

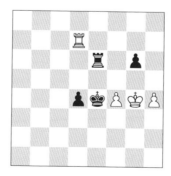

**56.h5?** And this even loses! After
the straightforward 56.♔g5 d3 57.h5
gxh5 58.f5 ♖e5 59.♔g6 ♖xf5 60.♖xd3
it's a simple draw.

**56...gxh5+ 57.♔xh5**

**57...♖f6!**
After this accurate move White can
no longer find his bearings.
**58.♔g5 ♖f5+ 59.♔g4 ♖xf4+
60.♔g3 ♖f5 61.♔g2 d3 62.♖e7+
♔d4 63.♖f7 ♖xf7**
And Black won.

## Conclusion
As we have seen from these games
against the younger generation, the
main issues they have seem to be
twofold:

**1** Their opening preparation is
based on preparing against their
next opponent, and not on a fully
integrated opening system. This
creates the possibility for older
players to use their age-proven
systems with well-rehearsed strategic plans to get serious advan-
tages in the middlegames.

**2** Their engine-based world forces
young players to focus more on
openings than on endgames.
The absence of adjournments has
put an end to the self-training
that players received when they
analysed their own games. They
simply rely on their capacity to
figure things out over the board.
During the last minute of the
game, when endgame positions
are played 'by hand', the older
generation profits from the fact
that they are accustomed to
noticing typical endgame tricks,
as we have much more experience with them. ∎

ARTHUR VAN DE OUDEWEETERING

# Struggling knights

## Sometimes a knight gets stranded on a square where it would rather not stay too long...

**H**ere's a typical example from the closed Ruy Lopez, where the queen's knight is often transferred to b7 on its way to a better life.

**Isaak Boleslavsky**
**Igor Bondarevsky**
Tbilisi 1951

**1.e4 e5 2.♘f3 ♘c6 3.♗b5 a6 4.♗a4 ♘f6 5.0-0 ♗e7 6.♖e1 b5 7.♗b3 0-0 8.c3 d6 9.h3 ♘a5 10.♗c2 c5 11.d4 ♕c7 12.♘bd2 cxd4 13.cxd4 ♗b7 14.d5 ♗c8 15.♘f1 ♘e8 16.b3 g6 17.♘e3 ♘g7 18.♗d2 ♘b7**

**19.♖c1 ♗d7 20.b4!** A standard move – and thus one to remember – to restrict the b7-knight. **20...♖ac8** 20...a5 21.a3 just gives White an extra target on b5, as in Bronstein-Geller, Soviet Union 1951, in which White eventually struck on the queenside. **21.♘g4 ♕d8** The wrong

plan. Boleslavsky recommended 21...f6 instead, so that the knight may go to f7 via d8. **22.♕e2**

**22...f5?** Black intends to launch an attack, but opening the position only helps White to restrict the off-side knight on b7. Boleslavsky finishes vigorously: **23.exf5 gxf5 24.♘h6+ ♔h8 25.g4!? ♕e8 26.gxf5 ♘xf5 27.♖xe5! ♘d4 28.♕e4 ♘xc2 29.♘xd7 ♘xe1 30.♘xf8 ♗xf8 31.♖xc8 ♕xc8 32.♕xe1 ♗g7 33.♕e6**

1-0.

Another regular opening that features a struggling knight ending up on b7 is this King's Indian line: 1.d4 ♘f6 2.♘f3 g6 3.g3 ♗g7 4.♗g2 0-0 5.c4 c5 6.♘c3 d6 7.0-0 ♘c6 8.d5 ♘a5. But less usual openings may leave the knight there as well, as witness the next example.

Anton Korobov
Richard Rapport
Abu Dhabi 2018

**1.d4 e6 2.c4 b6 3.a3 ♗b7 4.♘c3 ♘f6 5.♘f3 ♘e4 6.♘xe4 ♗xe4 7.♘d2 ♗g6 8.g3 ♘c6 9.e3 e5 10.d5 ♘a5 11.♗g2 ♗d6 12.b4 ♘b7**

**13.♗b2 a5 14.0-0 0-0 15.♕b3 ♕e7 16.♗c3 ♗d3 17.♖fc1 e4 18.♗f1 ♗xf1 19.♔xf1 ♖a7 20.♖ab1 axb4 21.axb4 ♖fa8 22.♕d1 f5 23.♔g2**

**23...♖a4?** 23...♘d8 24.♘b3, with the idea of c4-c5, suits White, but a4 turns out to be an awkward square for the rook. **24.♖a1! ♖a3** 24...♖xa1 25.♖xa1 ♖xa1 26.♕xa1 ♗xb4 27.♗xb4 ♕xb4 28.♕a8+ ♔f7 29.♕xb7 ♕xd2 30.♕xc7, and Black is in big trouble, since he will lose the d-pawn. **25.♖xa3** Korobov goes for a positional bind. Meanwhile, 25.♘b3 ♗xb4 26.d6! was a nice and strong tactic. **25...♖xa3 26.c5 bxc5 27.♘c4 ♖a8 28.b5 ♕f7 29.♖b1**

♗f8 30.b6 d6 31.bxc7 ♕xc7 32.g4 fxg4 33.♕xg4 ♖e8 34.♕h5 g6 35.♕h4 ♕f7?

**36.♕f6!** Exchanging the queens despite being a pawn down! But also eliminating the defender of the b7-knight. In general, when the active pieces disappear from the board, the remaining badly placed piece will hurt more. **36...♕xf6 37.♗xf6 ♗e7 38.♖xb7 ♗xf6 39.♘xd6** and Korobov converted this better end-game (1-0, 54).

Another Ruy Lopez line in which Black reckons the knight's outing to b7 will be temporary is 1.e4 e5 2.♘f3 ♘c6 3.♗b5 ♘f6 4.0-0 ♘xe4 5.d4 ♗e7 6.♕e2 ♘d6 7.♗xc6 bxc6 8.dxe5 ♘b7

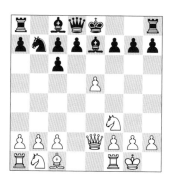

which leads to more open positions.

Here's an example from another opening.

**Vera Gonzalez Quevedo**
**Sergey Tiviakov**
Panama City 2013

1.d4 ♘f6 2.c4 e6 3.♘c3 ♗b4 4.♕c2 0-0 5.♘f3 c5 6.dxc5 ♘a6 7.g3 ♘xc5 8.♗g2 b6 9.0-0 ♗b7

## 'When the active pieces disappear from the board, the remaining badly placed piece will hurt more.'

**10.♘b5 ♗e4 11.♕d1 ♘b7** Completely different from the Ruy Lopez's above, but here, too, Black has to be careful not to overreach. **12.a3 ♗e7 13.♗f4 d6 14.♖c1 a6 15.♘c3 ♗c6**

**16.b4** Of course, again this move. The b7-knight will be doomed to passivity now. **16...♖c8 17.♕b3 ♘e4 18.♘xe4 ♗xe4 19.♘d2 ♗xg2 20.♔xg2 ♕d7 21.♖c2 d5 22.cxd5 ♖xc2 23.♕xc2 ♕xd5+? 24.e4 ♕d8 25.♖d1**

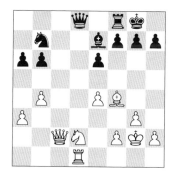

Again the exchange of pieces has left the b7-knight more conspicuous. The opening of the d-file was more than Black's position could take, and he duly lost after 25...a5 26.♘f3 ♕a8 27.♕c7 axb4 28.♕xe7 (1-0 in 56.)

**Bauer-Nijboer**
Nancy 2005
position after 19...♘b7

Time for a little controversy. This knight on b7 also looks horrible, doesn't it? Absolutely nowhere to go. Understandably, White opens the centre and exchanges some pieces. **20.f4 f5 21.♖e2 ♗xa1 22.♖xa1 ♕f6 23.♖ae1 ♖e7 24.e4 ♖be8 25.♗f2 a5 26.exf5 ♗xf5 27.♘e4 ♗d7! 28.♗f3 ♖xe2+ 29.♖xe2 ♖xe2+ 30.♕xe2 ♔f8**

Here Black's queen and bishop have more prospects than their counterparts, which compensates for the badly placed knight. White has no clear way to break through Black's position. Bauer's attempt to force matters now utterly backfired. **31.♘e4 ♕d4+ 32.♔g2 ♗f5 33.♘g5? h6** 33...♕d3!. **34.♘e6+ fxe6 35.dxe6 ♔e7 36.♗xb7 ♕d3 37.♕f2 ♕c2 38.♗c6 ♕h3+ 39.♔f3 ♕d3+ 40.♕e3 ♗g2+** 0-1.

So don't think the rest of the game will be plain sailing only because your opponent has a struggling knight. On the other hand, if it's your knight, it's generally advised not to have such a clumsy beast on b7! ∎

# In the mood

A proficient way to get into the right mood for a tournament, **MATTHEW SADLER** argues, is reading a good chess book or two. The various books that recently inspired our reviewer range from an entertaining collection of exercises to a wonderful memoir by the first wife of the great Mikhail Tal.

**A**pril is a time of holidays and the initial attempts of the sun to appear after months of gloom... even in the UK! However, for English chess players, April is also the lead-up to the final crucial weekend of the English 4NCL team competition at the start of May. I'm always praying that work will ease off and allow me to get a few evenings of chess work done. The month did start promisingly, but after a few consecutive nights spent working until 3 am, I lost the feeling of being a chess player again! However, a nice day spent watching the Grenke Classic on chess24 has got me back in the mood and some good books also help!

Before a tournament, I'm always on the lookout for good puzzle books. As a younger man, I might have tried my hand at *Oleg Pervakov's Industrial Strength Endgame Studies*, but I feared I might end up depressing myself by trying to solve studies by the most brilliant composer of our day just before a tournament, so *1001 Chess Exercises for Club Players* by Frank Erwich filled that gap nicely.

The book is divided up into 11 tactical themes, each introduced by a short explanation. The special feature of the presentation is that each diagram is accompanied by a hint such as 'luring' or 'chasing' (the exact meaning of these is defined in the book) which makes each puzzle just a little easier to solve.

I was very impressed by the range of positions that Erwich selected: I found myself muttering 'Oh that's nice' as I went through solving these positions (I've done about 400 so far), which is pretty good considering the number of such puzzles I've solved! I'll just give one slightly harder example from the chapter on Skewers. The hint for this puzzle was 'luring', which means 'forces a target to move to a bad square or line, most of the time by an exchange or a sacrifice, after which the position of the target can be exploited by a tactic'.

analysis position from
Giri-Carlsen, Shamkir 2018

**41...♕d5+ 42.♔g1 ♖f1+ 43.♔xf1 ♕h1+ 44.♔e2 ♕xh2+** wins the queen! Very neat, and just a little easier with a hint!
A good book of its kind! 4 stars!

■ ■ ■

*Checkmate – The love story of Mikhail Tal and Sally Landau* is the story of Mikhail Tal's first marriage to the actress Sally Landau, recounted both by Sally Landau herself and by Tal's son Gera Tal. You might say that the book is the film of Sally Landau's life with a huge starring role for Mikhail Tal! It's a strange book in some ways as Mikhail Tal's chess career plays just a small role in Sally's account. Sally wasn't a chess player and travelled little with him to tournaments as she was pursuing her own career and looking after their son Gera.

The book starts with an account of Sally's childhood and her first steps in her career as an actress, and, impatient to hear about Mikhail, I started to shift around restlessly on my chair as I read but... enter Mikhail Tal and I was hooked! Tal's games have been published the world over – many with his own fantastic, witty annotations – and there are many well-known stories about his heavy drinking and his amazing resilience in the face of so much illness, but this is the first time I have read anything about how he was as a person – as a son, as a husband and as a father. To be honest, he turned out perfectly as I would have wanted him to be – perhaps not an ideal husband

**1001 Chess Exercises for Club Players by Frank Erwich New In Chess, 2019**
★★★★☆

**Checkmate – The love story of Mikhail Tal and Sally Landau by Sally Landau Elk and Ruby, 2019**
★ ★ ★ ★ ★

or father, but certainly a character fitting the games that he played!

I am currently reading a biography of the phenomenal English concert pianist John Ogdon, and I couldn't help being struck by the similarities in the approach to life of two such geniuses. Just as Tal was renowned for the facility of his astonishing calculating ability, Ogdon was famous for his staggering ability to play even the most complicated and technically demanding music at sight. That amazing technical proficiency allowed both to move from seeing to executing faster than anyone else. Both Tal and Ogdon received enormous support from their family (although Tal's family seems much happier and warmer than Ogdon's was), every practical obstacle smoothed away by their mothers so they could focus on the expression of their genius. As Sally says about Tal, 'Misha didn't like problems – as an inwardly focused person they got in the way, and if they arose he genuinely believed that they should solve themselves. In any event, it wasn't down to him. Indeed, Robert and Ida [his parents] decided everything for him, especially Robert'.

Perhaps because of this focus, both had amazing stamina. When he (jointly) won the Tchaikovsky Piano Competition in 1962 (the most prestigious piano competition in the world), Ogdon returned in the middle of the competition from Russia to perform a piano concerto in London, returning to Russia straight after, to play the final: not a trivial undertaking in those days! Tal's son describes how in 1978, he accompanied his father to the USSR Team Championships. After three days, Tal's son realised that he couldn't keep up with Tal's rhythm, and had to leave. And remember: Tal's son wasn't even playing any chess! All-in-all, a wonderful addition to the Tal literature: 5 stars!

■ ■ ■

*Coach Yourself* (Everyman) is a new book by the English grandmaster Neil McDonald, since 2017 also an accredited FIDE trainer. Neil – a former Kent junior like myself – was a very prolific author in the early part of this century but this is the first book of his I have seen in a while. In the Introduction, McDonald states that 'the aim of this book is to show you everything you need to be working on to become a better player'. Every facet of the game gets some attention, as the following chapter titles indicate: 'Immunizing Yourself against Blunders', 'Learn How to Shut a Piece out of the Game', 'Wearing down the Opponent's Pawn Structure' and 'Making Good Opening Choices'.

I enjoyed this book: it has quite a relaxed, chatty pace to it, a little like having an informal session with an experienced player about certain important subjects which doesn't cost you too much effort as a reader, although it gets a little harder if you try to solve all the exercises McDonald sets you! I thought the chapter 'Know Yourself: Diagnosing Positional Mistakes' was particularly well thought-out. After an introduction in which McDonald analyses two similar mistakes he made in the British Championship of 1985(!),

he goes on to describe seven typical positional mistakes made by less experienced players (or strong players having a day off!):

1. Disregard of the Centre in an Eagerness to Attack
2. A Good-looking Idea Proves a Luxury You Can't Afford
3. Thoughtless Exchanges Release the Tension too Early
4. A Careless Pawn Move Weakens the King's Defences
5. Persisting with a Plan Your Pieces Can't Support
6. Failure to use Pawns
7. Criminal Passivity

All of these sections brought back some memories of mistakes – some my own, some of other players. I'll quote some of the section 'Failure to use Pawns' to give you an idea of the writing.

'At a recent international junior tournament, I went into the playing hall and saw one of my fellow chess coaches looking very content with life. His player as White had a healthy queenside pawn majority and a well-centralised king in a bishop versus knight endgame. White's plan was obvious: push the queenside pawns with the support of the bishop and king to create a passed pawn. This would virtually have decided the game.

'When I came back an hour and half later to look at the game, the player still had his queenside pawn majority... sitting on a2, b2, c3, with the bishop placed for safety in front of them on b3. Meanwhile, his opponent's king and knight were supporting a massive advance of Black's kingside pawn majority, which was about to break through on the sixth rank.'

Needless to say the game was soon lost for White and the coach was pulling his hair out. White had done nothing for the last 15 moves while his opponent had improved his game step by step. There are some players who are great at marking time and

## 'The book is the film of Sally Landau's life with a huge starring role for Mikhail Tal!'

cajoling their opponents into over-pressing (Ivanchuk, for example). But in most situations the opponent has useful moves to make, and that means you are going backwards.

It happens all the time that out of complacency ('my position is solid, there's no danger in not having a plan') or – the exact opposite – fear ('if I push my pawns, I'll weaken myself') a player drifts into passivity. McDonald then gives the following example to illustrate the dangers that await when a player does not want to touch his pawn structure.

**Belkhodja-Vaganian**
Moscow 2001
position after 26...♔f7

**27.♖d4** White can drive the black knight from its excellent post with 27.f4. I guess White didn't want to loosen his pawns with 27...gxf4 28.gxf4 nor expose his king to (an entirely harmless) check with 28...♘g6 29.♖xe7+ ♖xe7 30.♔f3 ♘h4+. In the game he pays a huge price for wanting to avoid even the ghost of a risk.
**27...♔f6 28.♖c2 h5** While White prevaricates, Vaganian improves his king and pawns.
**29.♘e2 g4 30.fxg4 hxg4 31.h4 ♘f3 32.♖d3 ♖e4 33.♖b2 ♖8e7 34.a4 a5 35.♘c3 ♖e1** And Black won easily.
An excellent, instructive read: 4 stars!

■ ■ ■

*Understanding before Moving 2 – Queen's Gambit Structures* by Herman Grooten (Thinkers Publishing) is the

**Coach Yourself**
**by Neil**
**McDonald**
**Everyman, 2019**
★★★★☆

next volume of Grooten's opening series following on from the book on the Ruy Lopez I reviewed before. This series is aimed squarely at the club player, aiming to convey a maximum of general understanding of typical structures and a minimum of opening theory, reinforced by model games and exercises. The concept is extremely attractive to amateur players: whatever your strength, it carries the promise of learning or revising some general strategic knowledge in an easy way. I feel however that the books – despite some instructive material – don't quite fulfil the promise of the concept.

The opening section on pawn structures covers the Carlsbad structure of the Queen's Gambit Declined:

and gives an uncomplicated and easy-to-read overview of both White's and Black's strategies in this structure. The plans described against the Minority Attack are not an exhaustive list, but I do like the attention that Grooten also gives to the plans with opposite-side castling. Since this is the only pawn structure examined,

**Understanding before**
**Moving 2 Queen's Gambit**
**Structures**
**by Herman Grooten**
**Thinkers Publishing, 2019**
★★★☆☆

I was expecting the theoretical section to focus on the Orthodox Queen's Gambit Declined. However, in contrast to the narrowness of the pawn structure section, this book's theoretical section covers all manner of Queen's Gambit openings such as the Tartakower, Lasker, Tarrasch, Noteboom and Vienna.

Each of these openings has a wide range of possible structures and you will never see a Carlsbad structure if you play the Vienna or the Tarrasch. I was therefore a little confused how these two sections linked into each other. Either a wider range of pawn structures should be considered in my view or the number of variations considered should be reduced. Also, considering how important early move orders are in Queen's Gambit openings, it feels a little strange to only see the starting moves 1.d4 d5 2.c4 e6 3.♘c3 examined in the theoretical section.

I guess that in terms of the execution of the book's concept, I'm not quite on the same wavelength as Grooten, so I should probably stop reviewing this series (though I will definitely keep on reading the bits I like!). For me the books are instructive but a little too diffuse in their content. Still, I'm sure that club players can learn some useful general strategical lessons from this book. 3 stars!

■ ■ ■

We conclude with *Unconventional Approaches to Modern Chess – Volume 1* by Alexander Ipatov (Thinkers Publishing). Rated 2650, Ipatov is best-known for his astonishing idea 1.d4 ♘a6 2.c4 e5

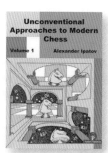

**Unconventional
Approaches to Modern
Chess Volume 1**
by Alexander Ipatov
**Thinkers Publishing**
★★★★★

(a sort of wonky Budapest), which he played against Sam Shankland at the St Louis Spring Chess Classic in 2018. As Ipatov relates, the story behind the novelty – conceived over the board – is just as funny as the move itself. Expecting Shankland to play 1.e4, Ipatov had prepared the offbeat line 1...c6 2.d4 ♘a6. After Shankland's unexpected 1.d4, 1...♘a6 seemed the logical reply to transpose back into his preparation after 2.e4. However, after 2.c4, Ipatov had to improvise, and the idea 2...e5 was born!

In retrospect, I wonder what Ipatov would have come up with after 2.♘f3? Perhaps 2...d5, with a wonky Chigorin? As you can see, Ipatov is not a player to follow the beaten track, and this book reflects this approach, offering a multitude of offbeat and lesser-known lines for Black against the entire range of White openings.

Just before looking at the chess, I must confess that I had somewhat mixed feelings about Ipatov's introduction to the book. Rather than learning and keeping up-to-date with main lines, Ipatov recommends preparing several less studied or neglected lines to cultivate 'predictable unpredictability'! He describes his philosophy as combatting several generally accepted misconceptions, such as a) only studying opening theory will make you a better player, b) one should always follow the first or second line shown by Komodo or Stockfish, and finally c) that 'in theory' is equivalent to 'over the board'. The last fallacy is especially dangerous because it implies that players will keep on making the best

moves over the board, and therefore sidelines should never be played as the opponent will always find a way to retain and convert the advantage. That is in theory. In practice however, many players will feel like a fish out of water once they end up in a position that is objectively better for them, but one that they have never analysed.'

I understand the approach, and I'm also sympathetic to this practical approach of chess, but I am sceptical that it cuts down the time you'll spend studying openings (especially when I seem to be holding a 350-page book packed with opening analysis!). When I started playing chess again around 2010 after about 9 years away from the game, I didn't fancy playing 10-year-old theoretical stuff that I only half-remembered, so I went totally offbeat with 1...a6, 2...h6 and all sorts of other stuff (including the 1.d4 ♘f6 2.c4 b6 line mentioned in the book). It was fun at the start, but gradually – burdened ever more by the awareness that the surprise effect had gone, and also with the growing understanding of all the annoying things that were wrong with the openings I was playing – I felt compelled to spend more and more time trying to patch them up. Before a game, I seemed to be spending ages nervously looking at my opponent's repertory and trying to second guess

what he would play prior to choosing a certain offbeat line. At some stage, I decided to switch back to main lines... to reduce the amount of opening work I had to do! With main lines, you always get a reasonable position and there are always lots of other people working on them, so problems tend to get fixed without requiring effort from you! Natasha Regan and I noticed something similar when we analysed the career opening choices of the late, great British player Tony Miles in our book *Chess for Life*. You saw clearly the negative effect that the database era had on Tony's openings choices (especially against 1.d4) as he struggled to find new offbeat openings to replace the ones that had lost their surprise effect.

So, I'm not convinced that this book will reduce the amount of opening work you'll have to do, but it will provide you with an awful lot of fun and inspiration! It isn't a complete repertoire book, but rather a collection of offbeat ideas (similar to the interesting book *Opening Originals* by David Lowinger (Russell Enterprises) which I reviewed some months back).

Against 1.e4, Ipatov covers original lines with 1...e5, 1...d6 (leading to the Philidor) 1...c6 and 1...c5. Against

# 'At some stage, I decided to switch back to main lines... to reduce the amount of opening work I had to do!'

1.d4, we see some Nimzo-Indian, 1...d6, 1...♘f6 and 2...b6, and 1...g6 before gradually moving on to some off-the-wall stuff like 1.♘f3 e6 2.c4 g5! (all played by very strong grandmasters!). In general, I think you'll use this book to spice up your current repertoire with a couple of additional interesting lines and possibly provide you with a one-off weapon for a must-win game. My rating for the book is somewhere between 4 and 5 stars, but Ipatov's generosity in sharing all this original analysis tips the balance to 5! Recommended! ∎

Jan Timman

# Magnus Carlsen reigns supreme

**The World Champion's devastating campaign in the Gashimov Memorial and the Grenke Classic also made a deep impression on JAN TIMMAN. 'An unparalleled performance', our honorary editor calls it.**

The past few months have been dominated by Magnus Carlsen. All other goings-on in the chess world were overshadowed by the World Champion's unparalleled performance in Shamkir, Karlsruhe and Baden-Baden. His two mega-victories in top tournaments in such quick succession are unique in chess history – no previous World Champion has pulled off a similar feat. Carlsen's achievement only gained in lustre in that he was in danger in only one game, against Ding Liren in Shamkir. Otherwise, the World Champion reigned supreme.

This inevitably leads to comments that his opponents always hit their worst form precisely when playing against him. This is not in itself incorrect, but it's part of a well-known phenomenon: the top player forces his own success. It already started in the second round against Anand.

**Magnus Carlsen**
**Vishy Anand**
Shamkir 2019 (2)

position after 28.♖xb1

In a Classical Queen's Gambit, White has not made much of the opening, and normally Anand would have had no problem saving the draw as Black, especially because he had more than 45 minutes left on his clock. But in Wijk aan Zee, Carlsen had beaten him from a dead-drawn position, and this must have made him nervous.

**28...♖c5?** A serious mistake. Black had several moves to stay in the fight. At the press conference, Anand indicated 28...♖a3, showing the following line: 29.a6 g6 30.♖b7 ♖a1+ 31.♔h2 ♖a2 32.♗b5 ♖a5, and White cannot capture the a-pawn. This variation can be deepened, because White does have a way to make progress: 33.♔g3 ♔g7 34.♗e2 ♖a2 35.♔f3, and now the a-pawn will eventually be lost regardless. But Black saves himself

with 35...d4 36.♖xa7 ♖a3!, and the d-pawn is suddenly strong.

Black, incidentally, had more moves to stay in the game, e.g. the passive 28...♖c7. He could also have gone 28...g5 to create space on the kingside, e.g. 29.♖b7 ♖c1+ 30.♔h2 ♖c2 31.♗b5 ♖xf2 32.♖xa7 d4, and Black has nothing to fear.

**29.a6** A reflex move that took Carlsen only one minute. If he had studied the position a bit longer, he would undoubtedly have seen that 29.♖b8+ first was the way to go. After 29...♔h7 30.a6 ♗c8, 31.♖b7 is devastating. Black cannot capture the white rook, because this would prevent his own rook from going to the b-file.

**29...g6** Another mistake. 29...♗c8 was called for here. After 30.♖b8 Black does not play his king to h7, because he would not have square b1 for his rook further on (because of the bishop check on d3). A good move is 30...g6, neutralising the threat of 31.♗g4.

**30.♖b7** White does not check the black king here, of course, because Black would just withdraw his bishop.

**30...♖c1+ 31.♔h2 ♖c2 32.♗b5 ♖b2 33.♔g3 ♗c8**

There is no other remedy; Black has to settle for a lost rook ending. 33...g5 would be met by 34.♗f1, and White wins.

**34.♖b8 ♔g7 35.♖xc8 ♖xb5 36.♖c7 ♖a5 37.♖xa7 ♔f6**

On ChessBase, Aryan Tari indicates 37...d4 as a better defence, and it is not a bad idea in itself to swap the weak d-pawn. But then White wins with 38.exd4 ♖d5 39.♖b7 ♖xd4 40.a7, and the king moves to the queenside unopposed.

**38.♖a8 ♖a3 39.♔h2 h5 40.a7**

This advance is usually not a good idea, for example if the black d-pawn was on e6. Here, however, it is completely justified, since the black d-pawn is weak and bound to fall.

**40...♖a2** During the press conference, Carlsen showed that 40...h4, trying to restrict the white king's elbow room, was equally hopeless in view of 41.g4 hxg3+ 42.fxg3, and Black cannot stop the white king from coming to the centre – via b1, if necessary. Black always finds himself in zugzwang, so that the king is

bound to capture the d-pawn in the end, after which the win is simple.

**41.h4 ♔f5 42.f3 ♖a1 43.g3**

Black resigned.

### Meeting again

Anand was the only player besides Carlsen who played in both the Gashimov Memorial and the Grenke Classic, with the result that the two World Champions faced off again exactly three weeks later – again with Carlsen as White. This time, something unusual happened: after working towards a winning position with superior play the World Champion failed to convert.

**Magnus Carlsen
Vishy Anand**
Karlsruhe/Baden-Baden 2019 (3)
English Defence, Smyslov Variation

**1.c4 e5 2.g3 ♘f6 3.♘c3 ♗b4 4.e4**

This advance is Vladimir Georgiev's brainchild, and Ferenc Berkes has also

# His achievement only gained in lustre in that he was in danger in only one game.

played it a few times. The idea is to be as flexible as possible while developing the kingside and try to dominate in the centre. Carlsen had played this against Caruana in London, so Anand had prepared for it.

**4...♗xc3** Probably the best move. Caruana played 4...0-0, but after 5.♘ge2 he found it hard to equalize.

**5.dxc3 d6** I played 5...♘xe4 here against Berkes in Paks 2010. But after 6.♕g4 ♘f6 7.♕xg7 ♖g8 8.♕h6 White is better, regardless of how interesting the position may be.

**6.f3** This is the idea. A Rossolimo with reversed colours has arisen, in which White is going to develop his king's bishop to d3.

**6...a5 7.♘h3 a4** A new move. In Svidler-Tomashevsky, Germany 2019, Black played 7...♘a6. This usually boils down to the same thing: the knight is *en route* to c5.

**8.♘f2 ♗e6 9.♗d3 ♘bd7 10.♕e2**

**10...c6**

Anand had played all his moves quite fast, and the text was basically flashed out as well. It is, however, a fairly serious mistake that saddles Black with a passive position without counterplay. 'I took my eye off the ball', said Anand afterwards.

Correct was the natural 10...♘c5 11.♗c2, which Carlsen would undoubtedly have met with 11...♘fd7 12.♘d1!, intending to cover the c-pawn from e3. The computer sees few problems for Black, but he will find it hard to create active counterplay.

**11.f4!** A powerful advance – the black pieces are misplaced. Anand thought for a long time.

**11...♘b6** Maybe 11...♘c5 would have offered better chances. After 12.♗c2 ♕c7 13.f5 ♗c8 14.♗g5, Black may try to create counterplay with 14...b5. But it doesn't look very reliable.

**12.♗e3 c5 13.0-0-0 ♕e7 14.f5 ♗d7 15.g4** Now Black will be overrun on the kingside.

**15...h6 16.h4 0-0-0 17.g5 ♘e8 18.♗d2 hxg5 19.hxg5 ♘c7 20.♘g4 ♖dg8 21.♖h2 ♕f8 22.♖dh1 ♔b8 23.b4 axb3 24.axb3 ♘c8 25.♔b2 ♕d8 26.♖h7 ♖xh7 27.♖xh7 ♖h8**

**28.♕h2**

Strange. Carlsen played the text almost at once, although he had more than 30 minutes on his clock.

The advance 28.g6 would probably

## 'I took my eye off the ball', said Anand afterwards.

have won, the idea being that White doesn't want to capture on g7 until his rook has an escape square. Black has the following options to try and defend himself:

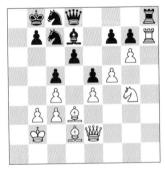

ANALYSIS DIAGRAM

– 28...fxg6 29.♖xg7 ♗e8 30.♗c2 of 30.♕f2, and Black's defence will fall short. White has all the time in the world to reinforce his position.

– 28...♖xh7 (the most tenacious move) 29.gxh7 ♕h8 30.♕h2 f6 31.b4 ♘b6 32.♗e3 or 32.♘e3, and White should be winning. It's a very depressing position for Black with the queen as a permanent blocking piece. Yet White will not find it easy to break through, because the position keeps its closed character. We don't know why Carlsen did not advance the g-pawn, because he was not present at the post-round press conference.

**28...♖xh7 29.♕xh7 ♕f8 30.♘e3 ♘e7 31.♔c2**

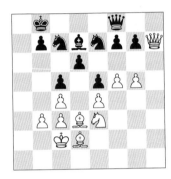

White still has a large advantage. The text is the start of a king-march to f2, which is definitely a better place for it if White wants to set his b-pawn moving.

**31...♕g8 32.♕h4 ♕f8 33.♔d1 ♘c6 34.♕h7 ♘e7 35.♔e2 ♘c8 36.♔f2 ♘e7 37.♗e2 ♕g8 38.♕h1**

More accurate was 38.♕h4, intending to meet 38...g6 with 39.♗d3, and the g-pawn continues to be protected.

**38...g6!**

An excellent defensive move that closes the kingside.

**39.♕h6 ♘e8**

Protecting the d-pawn. Now White is forced to advance his f-pawn.

**40.f6 ♘c6 41.b4 ♘c7 42.bxc5 dxc5 43.♘d5 ♘e6**

Black has his line of defence in order.

**44.♗e3 ♚a7**

A rather strange move, but it just about works. More natural was 44...♕d8, intending to meet 45.♕h7 with 45...♕f8.

**45.♗g4 b6 46.♘c7 ♕c8 47.♘b5+ ♚b8 48.♘d6**

**48...♕g8**

It was not easy to see, but Black could have made a queen sortie here with 48...♕a6. After 49.♘xf7 ♕a2+ 50.♗e2 both 50...♘ed4 and 50...♘f4 would create sufficient counterplay for Black. The white f-pawn is not very strong yet.

**49.♕h1 ♕f8**

**50.♕d1**

This queen move allows Black to regroup, which would have been slightly more difficult after 50.♘b5. After 50...♗c8 51.♕d1 ♘a7 52.♕d6+ ♕xd6 53.♘xd6 ♘d8 Black's defensive line is still intact. An interesting variation now is 54.♗f5 ♚c7 55.♘xf7

A remarkably relaxed post-mortem after Magnus Carlsen had let Vishy Anand off the hook in a tense game at the Grenke Classic.

♘xf7 56.♗xg6 ♗e6 57.♗h5 ♘c8 58.g6 ♘cd6, and Black maintains his blockade.

**50...♘cd8 51.♘b5 ♗c6 52.♔g1**

**52...♘c7**

Anand is getting tired. 52...♗xb5 53.cxb5 ♚c7 would have been an easy way to create a blockade, as he indicated after the game. The text is based on a simple miscalculation.

**53.♗f2!**

A strong little move. The bishop is heading for g3, after which it will be virtually impossible to protect the black e-pawn.

**53...♘b7** Black had planned 53...♘xb5 54.cxb5 ♗xe4 55.♗g3 ♕h8, but his counterplay comes too late. 56.♗xe5 is mate in four, and 56.♕d6+ is equally devastating.

**54.♗g3 ♗xb5 55.cxb5 ♕d6**

**56.♕e2** Played after a five-minute think. Carlsen must have been disappointed about allowing his advantage to evaporate, and fails to grab this new chance.

The text relieves the pressure on the black position. Anand had rightly been in fear of 56.♔g2, because a queen swap would do Black no good. After 56...♕xd1 57.♗xd1 ♘xb5 58.♗xe5+ ♚c8 59.♗e2, White has a winning endgame.

**56...♘e6**

Suddenly, Black has everything back under control. He is not worse at all.

**57.♗xe6** 57.♕h2 would be met by 57...♘f4 58.♕a2 ♕d3!, with sufficient counterplay.

Another option was 57.♕c4, but after 57...♘xg5 58.♕d5 ♕xd5 59.exd5 ♘d6 60.♗xe5 ♚c7 Black has a perfect blockade.

**57...♕xe6 58.♕h2 ♕g4 59.♔f2**
**♕xe4 60.♗xe5+ ♔c8 61.♕h3+**
**♔d8 62.♕h8+ ♔d7 63.♕h3+**
**♔d8** Draw.

### The Sveshnikov

Back to Shamkir. In Round 3, Carlsen managed to win his second game with his current pet line of the Sicilian: the Sveshnikov.

**David Navara**
**Magnus Carlsen**
Shamkir 2019 (3)

position after 14...f5

This position arose after slightly more than 20 minutes. It is likely that both players were still in their preparation.

**15.♘c4** Navara played this pretty fast as well. White wants to increase the pressure on the centre. But the computer has a clear preference for 15.♘b5, after which it assesses the position as better for White. And it's true that on b5 the knight has a strong and unassailable foothold.
**15...b6 16.♖a3 exf4 17.♗xf4 ♘c5**

**18.♖e3** 'A blunder', opined Carlsen. Navara thought about it for only two minutes. A different rook move was the correct one: 18.♖g3. The position is dynamically balanced, e.g. 18...♘xa4 19.♘xd6 ♗xd6 20.♕d4 ♕f6 21.♕xa4 ♗xf4 22.♕xf4 ♕xb2 23.♕c7 ♖f7 24.♕d8+, with perpetual check.
**18...g5!** Not so hard to find. Other moves would give White a large advantage. **19.♖xe7 gxf4**

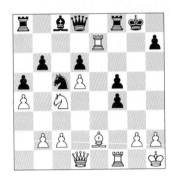

It turned out that Navara, in his calculations, had overlooked that his rook has no squares now.
**20.♖e6** Trying to make the best of it.
**20...♘xe6 21.dxe6 ♗xe6 22.♖xf4 ♗xc4 23.♗xc4+ ♔h8 24.g4** This is the best try. **24...♕f6 25.c3 ♕e5 26.♕f1 ♖ae8 27.gxf5 ♖f6 28.♕f2 ♕c5 29.♔g2**

**29...♕c6+** Some slight hesitation. Black could have swapped the queens here, and 29...♖ef8 was also very strong. After 30.♕xc5 dxc5 31.♗d3 ♖d6 32.♗c4 ♔g7 Black has a technical win.
**30.♔h3** A more tenacious defence was 30.♔g3, after which 30...♖e7 is the best move (not 30...♕c5, as in the game, in view of 31.♗e6, and White will survive). After 31.♖g4 d5 32.♗d3 ♖g7 Black will just about succeed in getting a technically winning position.

**30...♕c5** Carlsen decides to go for repetition, which, technically speaking, is the best move.
**31.♔g2** White cannot take his bishop to e6 now, since this would leave his queen insufficiently defended.
**31...♕xf2+ 32.♖xf2 ♖e4 33.♗e6 ♖xa4 34.♔f3 ♔g7 35.♖d2 ♔h6 36.♖xd6 ♔g5 37.♖d8** After 37.♖xb6 ♖f4+ 38.♔e3 ♖4xf5 Black wins easily. **37...♔h6 38.♖g8+ ♔f6 39.♖b8 ♖xh2 40.♖xb6 ♔g5 41.f6 ♖f4+ 42.♔g3 ♖hf2 43.♖b5+ ♔xf6 44.♗g4 a4 45.c4 ♔g6 46.c5**

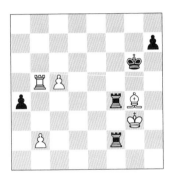

**46...a3** 46...h5 would have yielded Black a more convincing win, but this required extremely sharp calculations that would be very hard to find over the board. The main line goes as follows: 47.♗xh5+ ♔xh5 48.c6+ ♔h6! 49.c7 ♖4f3+ 50.♔g4 ♖f8 51.♖b8 ♖g2+ 52.♔h3 ♖gg8, and now the point of move 48 is revealed: the g-file had to be opened. Black is winning.
**47.bxa3 h5 48.♖b4** Now 48.♗xh5+ would lose simply because of 48...♔xh5 49.c6+ ♔g6 50.c7 ♖2f3+ and the rook gets to c3. That's why Carlsen sacrificed his a-pawn – to get the c3-square.
**48...♖f8 49.♗d1**

**49...⬛d2** An important technical move.
**50.⬛f3 ⬛d3 51.⬛f4 h4+ 52.⬛g4 ⬛xf4+ 53.⬛xf4 ⬛xa3**
The Norwegian IM and endgame study composer Geir Ostmoe pointed out in a tweet that the position with the black king on h6 instead of on g6 would be a draw. In that case, the black king would be too far away from the white c-pawn.
**54.c6 ⬛c3 55.⬛d5** With the black king on h6 White could have withdrawn his bishop to g2, in order to sacrifice it for the h-pawn. The white king is then in time to support the c-pawn via e5.
**55...h3 56.⬛e5**

**56...⬛c5!** The only winning move.
**57.⬛d6 ⬛xd5+ 58.⬛xd5 h2**
White resigned.

**In the style of Kasparov**
After this win the machine stalled a bit. Three times in a row, Carlsen got no more than a draw. But it was the prelude to a final winning streak. In Round 7 he played Giri – a prestige battle. In their 21 games, the World Champion could boast only a minimal plus score against the Dutch crack, after having looked at a minus score for years. Carlsen was extra motivated, and chess fans certainly weren't disappointed. He played an attacking game in the style of Kasparov.

**Magnus Carlsen**
**Anish Giri**
Shamkir 2019 (7)
English Opening, Reversed Dragon
**1.c4 e5 2.⬛c3 ⬛f6 3.⬛f3 ⬛c6 4.g3 d5 5.cxd5 ⬛xd5 6.⬛g2 ⬛c5**
This bishop development has been the great rage since Grischuk introduced it two years ago.

**7.0-0 0-0 8.d3 h6**
Not new, but only played once before in a game between unknown players. The usual move is 8...⬛e8, which is what Caruana played.
**9.⬛xd5 ⬛xd5 10.a3**

## Carlsen was extra motivated, and chess fans certainly weren't disappointed.

The alternative is 10.b3, aiming for a double fianchetto.
**10...a5 11.⬛d2 ⬛e6 12.⬛c1**

**12...⬛e7**
It is not certain that Black was right to withdraw his queen here. Another option was 12...⬛b6, e.g. 13.⬛c3 ⬛d4 14.e3 ⬛xf3+ 15.⬛xf3 c6, with roughly equal chances.
**13.⬛c3 ⬛d4 14.e3 ⬛xf3+ 15.⬛xf3 ⬛d6 16.⬛h5 c6**
After the game Carlsen indicated 16...f5 as stronger, but it doesn't seem to make any difference. After 17.f4 Black has nothing better than 17...c6.

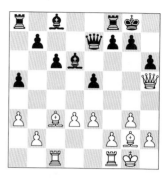

**17.f4!** A deeply calculated pawn sacrifice. **17...exf4** Black picks up the gauntlet. With 17...f5 he could have maintained the central balance, although 18.⬛ce1 ⬛d7 19.⬛h1 would have left White slightly better.
**18.gxf4!** The point of the previous move. Carlsen wants to use the half-open g-file for an attack.

**18...⬛xe3+**
Far too dangerous. Accepting the pawn sacrifice costs precious time. He could have justified his previous move with the hidden king move 18...⬛h7!, after which White has the following possibilities:

ANALYSIS DIAGRAM

– The sharpest move is 19.f5, revealing the point of Black's 18th

Anish Giri paid dearly for accepting Magnus Carlsen's deeply calculated pawn sacrifice.

move: there follows 19...♕xe3+ 20.♔h1 ♕g5, and the white attack is slowed down. The position is dynamically balanced, as witness the following spectacular line: 21.♕h3 ♖e8 22.♖g1! (22.♗e4 is harmless in view of 22...♗e5!, and Black is better) 22...♕xf5! 23.♗e4 ♕xe4+! (the point of the previous move) 24.dxe4 ♗xh3 25.♖xg7+ ♔h8 26.♖g5+!, with perpetual check.

– 19.e4 g6 20.♕e2 ♗e6 21.♔h1 (21.♖ce1 is met strongly by 21...♕h4) 21...f5 22.e5 ♗c7, with a solid position.

**19.♔h1**

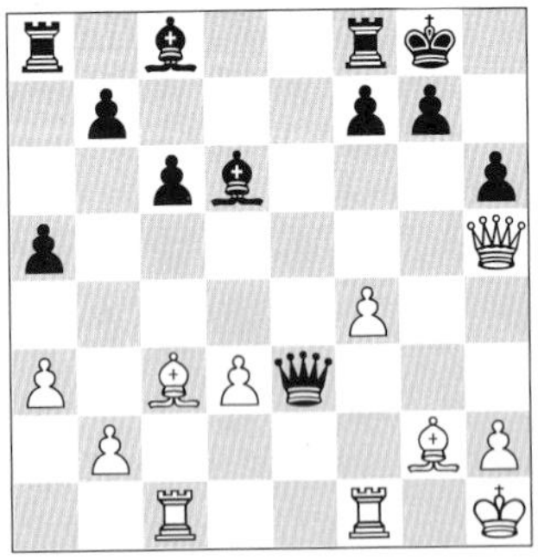

**19...♖d8**

Intending to withdraw the bishop to f8. But this plan cannot slow down the white attack. Black's only chance was 19...f6, blocking the white queen's bishop's diagonal. White gets a dangerous attack with 20.♗e4 ♕h3 21.♕g6, but now the black king can flee to the queenside as follows: 21...♗g4 22.♕h7+ ♔f7 23.♗g6+ ♔e6 24.♖ce1+ ♔d7 25.♕xg7+ ♔c8 26.♗e4 ♕h5, and although Black's position is dubious, there is no forced win for White.

**20.♖ce1 ♕c5 21.f5**

This advance cuts off both the enemy queen and its bishop.

**21...♗f8**

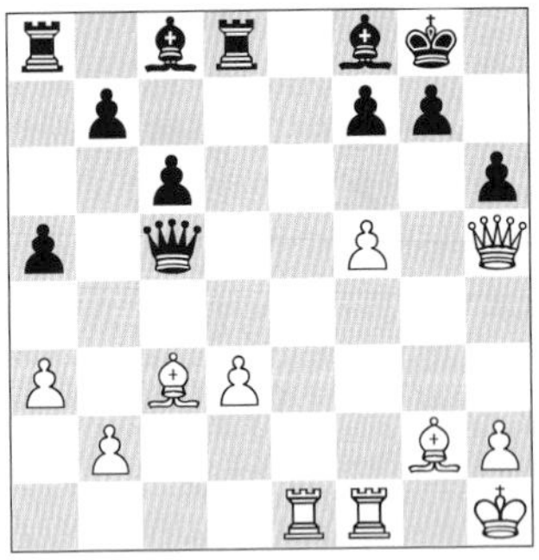

**22.♗e4** The logical continuation of the attack. White gives his f-pawn extra support in order to be able to take his rook to g1.

The alternative 22.♖e5 was also winning, its point becoming clear after 22...♕d6 23.♗e4 f6 24.♕g6!. Black cannot capture the rook, because that would grant the f-pawn a decisive breakthrough. And 24...♕c7 is met devastatingly by 25.♖e6!.

**22...♖d5 23.♖f3 b5**

Both players had seen that 23...g6 would run into an elegant refutation: 24.fxg6 ♕xc3 25.gxf7+ ♔h8 26.♖g1, with mate to follow.

**24.♖g1 ♖a7 25.♗f6 g6**

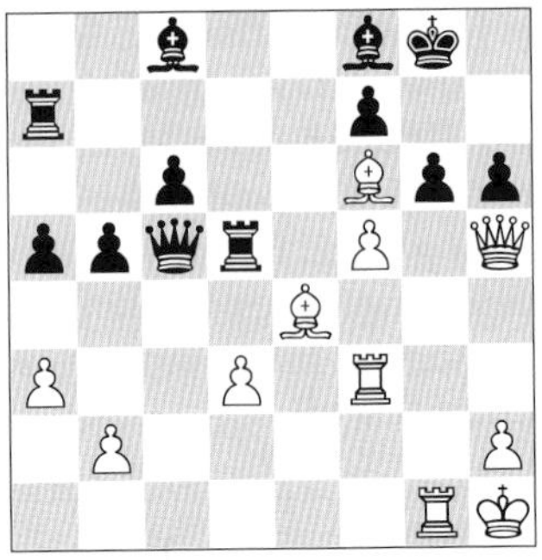

**26.♕h3** In general Carlsen is not aiming to get brilliancy prizes. With 26.♖xg6+! he could have decided the game in style. The point of the rook sac becomes clear after 26...fxg6 27.♕xg6+ ♗g7 28.♗c3!. The subtle bishop move opens the way for the f-pawn. After 28...b4, 29.f6 is decisive.

**26...♖d6** After 26...b4 White would withdraw his queen, 27.♕f1, after which the capture on g6 is a certainty.

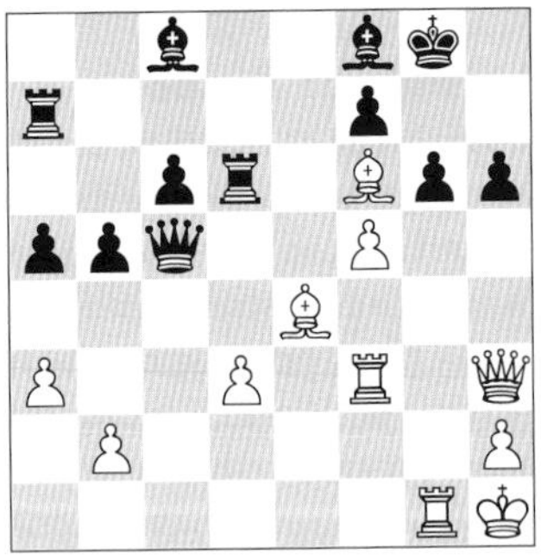

**27.♕h4** White decides to go for a technically winning endgame. With 27.d4 he could have won in the attack, as witness the following main line: 27...♖xd4 28.fxg6 ♗xh3 (if 28...fxg6 then the devastating 29.♖xg6+) 29.gxf7+ ♔xf7 30.♗xd4+, and wins.

**27...♖xf6 28.♕xf6 ♗e7 29.♕xc6 ♕xc6 30.♗xc6 ♔g7 31.fxg6 fxg6 32.d4 a4**

Giri was in serious time-trouble, which makes it impossible to create saving attempts. With 32...♗d6

33.♗d5 ♖e7 he could have tested White's technique.

**33.d5 b4**

**34.♗e8! ♗g5 35.h4 ♗xh4 36.♖xg6+ ♔h7 37.♖c6 ♗g4 38.♖f4 ♖g7** Black resigned.

How Carlsen won his final two games in excellent style, you can find elsewhere in this issue.

### Impressive chess erudition

The Grenke Classic started with a game I was looking forward to with great interest: Keymer-Carlsen, which is annotated by the white player elsewhere in this issue. What struck me was that White was surprised by Black's 13th move, which convinced me that he had not read my book *Timman's Titans*, in which I discuss a fragment from Bronstein-Petrosian, 1956 Candidates, at some length.

**David Bronstein**
**Tigran Petrosian**
Leeuwarden 1956

position after 17.♘h3

In this position, Petrosian played:
**17...♗xc3 18.bxc3 ♘f6** with a

good position. This is exactly the plan Carlsen followed against Keymer.
**19.a4 ♔h8 20.♘f2 ♖g8 21.♔h1 ♕e8 22.♖g1 ♕g6 23.♕d2 ♗d7 24.g3 ♖ae8 25.a5 ♖e7 26.♖ab1 ♗c8 27.♖g2 ♖eg7 28.♖bg1 ♘ce8 29.h3 h5** Draw.

Later, the same swap on c3 occurred in two more games, which I also discuss in the book: Donner-Petrosian, Santa Monica 1966, and Timman-Tal, Tallinn 1973, each time in a slightly different version. Carlsen has read my book; in an interview in *Straits Times* he had nothing but praise for it. So he swapped on c3 with barely a thought, relying on Petrosian's and Tal's strategic judgment.

But even if Carlsen had not read my book, he would probably have known those games by his predecessors. He is impressively erudite chess-wise. This is part of the basis of his success. I also think he has learnt much from the book *Game Changer*, published during the Tata tournament. It is probably not a coincidence that Carlsen started his glorious winning streak roughly from the moment he had laid eyes on that book; the greatest talents always profit the most from new developments.

In Round 2, Carlsen struck again.

**Paco Vallejo**
**Magnus Carlsen**
Karlsruhe/Baden-Baden 2019 (2)

position after 30...♖d8

The position is equal, but Vallejo was in time-trouble. One of Carls-

## Carlsen started his winning streak roughly from the moment he had laid eyes on Game Changer.

en's strong points is that he always manages his time very economically.
**31.f4+**
During the press conference, Carlsen revealed that he had completely overlooked this move in his calculations. Fortunately, there wasn't much to it.
**31...gxf3** Black could have sacrificed a piece with 31...♘xf4 32.gxf4+ ♔xf4. The black pawn front is strong, so he has enough compensation. A possible follow-up is: 33.♗c2 ♖d2 34.♗e2 ♖xe2 35.♔xe2 b5, and a draw is in the offing. There is little doubt that Carlsen was playing to win at this stage.
**32.♗xf3** Certainly not 32.h4+, because then Black is certain to sacrifice a piece: 32...♘xh4! 33.gxh4+ ♔f4, and White will be mated.
**32...h4**

**33.♘c4**
This was probably the worst position Carlsen had in the Grenke Classic. Instead of the cautious text, White could have gone 33.♗xb7 to keep his initiative. He need not fear the invasion of the black rook. After 33...♖d2 34.♘c6 ♗c5 35.♔e1 ♖xh2 36.♘d8! White threatens to corner the black king. Black scrapes through with 36...♔h6.

**33...hxg3 34.hxg3 ♗b8 35.♔g2 b5 36.axb5 axb5 37.♘e3**

A typical time-trouble move. 37.♘a3 f4 38.♗e4 would have removed all danger.

**37...♖d2+ 38.♔h3**

**38...♖d3** Black is creating winning chances. **39.♗e2 ♖xc3 40.♗xb5 f4 41.♗e8 ♘f8 42.♖b6 ♗e5 43.♘f1 fxg3 44.♖c6 ♖a3 45.♖b6 ♖a2 46.♖b4 ♘e6 47.♖g4+ ♔f6**

**48.♗c6**

The decisive error; White is forced into a theoretically lost endgame.
He should have aimed for a different theoretical endgame with 48.♖xg3. After 48...♗xg3 White has two ways to capture the bishop:

ANALYSIS DIAGRAM

– 49.♔xg3 ♘g7 50.♗d7! (the only move – the black knight must be kept from f5) 50...♔g5, and now both 51.♘e3 and 51.♔f3 are sufficient to draw. White should centralize as much as possible.
– 49.♘xg3? would lose, since it leaves the king on the edge. Black's optimal move is 49...♔g5, with mate in 28. Remarkably enough, the second best move, 49...♘d4, leads to mate in 103(!). And there are eight more winning moves with mate in well over 100 moves.

**48...g2!**

Vallejo must have underestimated this vicious little move.

**49.♗xg2 ♘f4+ 50.♖xf4+ ♗xf4**

A theoretically winning endgame has arisen. 'I guess you get this once in your life and this is my turn,' Carlsen observed afterwards. I myself have never had this endgame, but on one particular occasion I was a witness to it: it occurred in Nikolic-Kortchnoi, Tilburg 1987, when it was not yet known that it was theoretically winning. 'Normally it should be a draw,' Nikolic observed in his comments for New In Chess 1988/1. I remember having serious doubts about this assessment. It seemed to me that the presence of opposite-coloured bishops should eventually yield the player with the rook a winning attack. This assessment was

later confirmed by the computer. Nikolic had a good starting position and managed to win in 30 moves. In Karlsruhe, the starting position was less advantageous for Black: it is mate in 55. This means that Black would probably just have made it under the 50-move rule, because a white piece is taken shortly before the mate. Carlsen was not sure and asked the arbiter: 'How many moves do I have?' – because not so long ago, you had 75 moves for certain endgames. In the 1980s, you even got 100 moves for the endgame of rook+bishop vs. rook because of the Philidor position. After vehement protests the rule was scrapped. At the moment, there is a great number of theoretical endgames in which the win requires more than 50 moves – I will only mention the endgame of rook+knight vs. bishop+knight that I just discussed. For this reason, not a single exception is made, which is what the arbiter told the World Champion. The game continued.

**51.♗f3 ♗b8 52.♘g3 ♔g5 53.♘e2**
The only move to prevent mate. White throws up a blockade with knight and bishop that keeps the black king away for a long time.
**53...♗c7 54.♔g2 ♔h4 55.♔f2 ♗b6+ 56.♔e1 ♗e3 57.♔d1**

**57...♔g5** Up to this moment, Carlsen has demonstrated a phenomenal feel for the endgame: all his moves are the optimal choices. But this one slows the win by seven moves. The optimal way was 57...♖d2+ 48 58.♔e1 ♖d8, which is relatively obvious. 'I was seeing ghosts,' said Carlsen

**Once again working late. On an otherwise deserted stage, Magnus Carlsen ground down Paco Vallejo in a complicated endgame.**

afterwards. But I think he deliberately opted for the text in view of his plan to take his king to the queenside. The reason? There is an interesting situation that strikes the eye most clearly if White puts his bishop on e4: the position is symmetrical on both sides of the e-file, and this shows that the king has less room on the kingside. So if Black takes his king to the queenside, he seems to have a better chance of forcing the enemy king to the kingside. It's a very reasonable thought, but it still doesn't seem to work this way.

**58.♗e4 ♔f6** Black continues with his plan, but again the manoeuvre 58...♖d2+ 59.♔e1 ♖d8 was optimal.
**59.♗f3 ♔e5 60.♗g2 ♔d6 61.♗e4 ♔c5 62.♗f5 ♖d2+ 63.♔e1 ♖d8 64.♗e4 ♔c4**

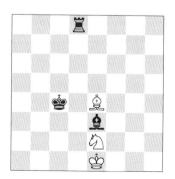

**65.♔f1** If Vallejo had played 65.♘g3, it is doubtful that Carlsen would have made it within the 40 moves he had left, because that makes it mate in 58. The text allows Black to progress more quickly.
**65...♖f8+ 66.♔e1**
More tenacious was 66.♔g2, with the point that Black cannot take the knight after 66...♖f2+ 67.♔h1 in view of 68.♗d3+!, and stalemate. He will have to withdraw his bishop with 67...♗a7, after which it is mate in 39, just within the 50-move limit.
**66...♗f2+**
Carlsen now finishes the game in exemplary fashion. He chases the enemy king to the queenside, where it will be caught in a mating net.
**67.♔d2 ♖d8+ 68.♔c2 ♗e3 69.♗f3 ♖d2+ 70.♔b1 ♔b3 71.♘c1+ ♔a3 72.♘e2 ♖b2+ 73.♔a1 ♖b8**
White resigned.

His two marathon battles must have tired Carlsen, because they were followed by another impasse: three consecutive draws. But it took nothing away from his impressive final four-win streak in Baden-Baden. ∎

# Robert Hess

CURRENT ELO: **2581**

DATE OF BIRTH: **December 19, 1991**

PLACE OF BIRTH: **New York City, USA**

PLACE OF RESIDENCE: **New York City, USA**

**What is your favourite city?**
My hometown ☺.

**What was the last great meal you had?**
Armenian barbecue with WGM Tatev Abrahamyan and her relatives overlooking Lake Sevan, Armenia.

**What drink brings a smile to your face?**
Pineapple juice.

**Which book would you give to a friend?**
*Invisible Man* by Ralph Ellison.

**What book is currently on your bedside table?**
Never just one! *Zeitoun* (Dave Eggers), *Mind and Matter* (John Urschel & Louisa Thomas), *Born a Crime* (Trevor Noah).

**What is your all-time favourite movie?**
*The Silence of the Lambs.*

**And your favourite TV series?**
I have pretty varied taste, but to pick two: *Twin Peaks* and *BoJack Horseman*.

**Do you have a favourite actor?**
I'd watch anything with Robin Williams.

**And a favourite actress?**
Mireille Enos.

**What music do you listening to?**
Leon Bridges. And always Creedence Clearwater Revival.

**Is there a work of art that moves you?**
*Portrait of Jeanne Kéfer* by Fernand Khnopff.

**What is your earliest chess memory?**
My dad teaching me and my siblings how to play.

**Who is your favourite chess player?**
GM Miron Sher. He instilled in me a love for the game and is the best coach a person could ever ask for.

**Is there a chess book that had a profound influence on you?**
*Endgame Strategy* by Shereshevsky.

**What was your best result ever?**
2nd at the 2009 U.S. Championship.

**And the best game you played?**
Nakamura-Hess, Foxwoods 2009.

**What is your favourite square?**
e5.

**Do chess players have typical shortcomings?**
An obsession with chess ☺.

**What are chess players particularly good at (except for chess)?**
They tend to have good memories.

**Do you have any superstitions concerning chess?**
Not at all, though I've always enjoyed taking walks before my games.

**Facebook, Instagram, Snapchat, or?**
In-person conversation.

**How many friends do you have on Facebook?**
2599.

**What is your life motto?**
Efficiency is intelligent laziness.

**When were you happiest?**
Wizarding World of Harry Potter with my siblings. Pure bliss.

**When was the last time you cried?**
Watching *Coco*.

**Which three people would you like to invite for dinner?**
Muhammad Ali, Queen Elizabeth I, Jordan Peele.

**What is the best piece of advice you were ever given?**
'Be yourself; everyone else is already taken' – Oscar Wilde.

**Is there something you'd love to learn?**
Spanish.

**What would people be surprised to know about you?**
I'm a very good dodgeball player!

**Where is your favourite place in the world?**
Kyoto, Japan.

**What is your greatest fear?**
Quicksand.

**And your greatest regret?**
That can't be published!

**If you could change one thing in the chess world, what would it be?**
More interaction between players and fans/more media training.

**Is a knowledge of chess useful in everyday life?**
Maybe every other day.

**What is the best thing that was ever said about chess?**
I'm not even sure if this is a real quote, but 'There just isn't enough televised chess' – David Letterman.